Facilitation
at a Glance!

4th Edition

Ingrid Bens

Published by GOAL/QPC
The Memory Jogger Company

Your Pocket Guide to Facilitation

Facilitation at a Glance! — Fourth Edition
Your Pocket Guide to Facilitation

All of the features that made past editions so popular have been retained in the 4th edition, and a number of new elements have been added. There is a new chapter about the art of questioning that helps facilitators identify the right questions to ask in a wide variety of situations. The chapters on decision making and conflict management have been revised to add important new techniques. In the fourth edition, the chapter on meeting management now features process notes for the all important Status Update Meeting. The same chapter also includes at a glance charts describing facilitator best practices, before, at the start, during and at the end of every meeting. With this new edition, Facilitation at a Glance! retains its importance as a must-have resource for anyone who plans meetings or leads teams.

Author: Ingrid Bens, M.Ed.
Design and Editing: GOAL/QPC

GOAL/QPC
13 Branch Street, Suite 103, Methuen, MA 01844
800.643.4316 or 603.893.1944
service@goalqpc.com

www.GOALQPC.com

Printed in the United States of America | Fourth Edition

ISBN: 978-1-57681-183-2

10 9 8 7 6 5 4 3 2

TABLE OF CONTENTS

11 —Meeting Design Template

Introduction

It's impossible to be part of an organization today and not attend meetings. Staff meetings, project meetings, task force meetings, planning and coordinating meetings…the list is endless. The worst thing about many of these meetings is that they're poorly run and waste valuable time.

Today, there's been a growing recognition that effective meetings happen when proper attention has been paid to the process elements and when proceedings are skillfully facilitated.

We're now spending so much time in meetings and being asked to achieve so many important goals in teams that there's a growing need for skilled facilitation throughout our organizations and our communities.

 With its focus on asking instead of telling, listening, and building consensus, facilitation is the essential skill for anyone working collaboratively with others.

Facilitation is fast becoming a core competency for anyone who leads a team, manages a project, heads up a committee, or manages a department. To get the most from people today, leaders have to know how to create buy-in, generate participation, and empower people.

To keep pace, today's leaders need to be coaches, mentors, and teachers. At the core of each of these new roles is the skill of facilitation.

— *Ingrid Bens*, M.Ed., CPF

KEY DEFINITIONS

> **Facilitator:** One who contributes structure and process to interactions so groups are able to function effectively and make high-quality decisions. A helper and enabler whose goal is to support others as they pursue their objectives.

- **Content:** The topics or subjects under discussion at any meeting. Also referred to as the task, the decisions made, or the issues explored.

- **Process:** The structure, framework, methods, and tools used in interactions. Also refers to a climate or spirit established, as well as the style of the facilitator.

- **Intervention:** An action or set of actions that aims to improve the functioning of a group.

- **Plenary:** A large group session held to share the ideas developed in separate subgroups.

- **Norms:** A set of rules created by group members with which they mutually agree to govern themselves.

- **Group:** Individuals who come together to share information, coordinate their efforts, or achieve a task, but who mainly pursue their own individual goals and work independently.

 Facilitation at a Glance! | Fourth Edition | ©2018 GOAL/QPC

- **Team:** A collection of individuals who are committed to achieving a common goal, who support each other, who fully utilize member resources, and who have closely linked roles.

- **Process Agenda:** A detailed step-by-step description of the tools and techniques used to bring structure to conversations.

- **Project:** A collaborative enterprise, frequently involving research or design, that is carefully planned to achieve a particular aim.

- **Process Improvement:** A series of actions taken by a process owner to identify, analyze, and improve existing processes within an organization to meet new goals and objectives.

- **Lean:** A practice that considers the expenditure of resources for any goal other than the creation of value for the end customer to be wasteful, and thus a target for elimination. Basically, lean is centered on preserving value with less work.

- **Six Sigma:** A business management strategy that seeks to improve the quality of process outputs by identifying and removing the causes of defects or errors and minimizing variability. A six sigma process is one in which 99.99966 percent of the products manufactured are statistically expected to be free of defects (3.4 defects per million).

THE FACILITATOR'S GREATEST CONTRIBUTION IS TO PROVIDE STRUCTURE SO THAT PARTICIPANTS CAN FOCUS ON MAKING THE BEST DECISIONS POSSIBLE.

Chapter ONE

Understanding Facilitation

Facilitation is a way of proving leadership without taking the reins. A facilitator's job is to enable others to assume responsibility and take the lead.

 Facilitation is a helping role.

What Does a Facilitator Do?

Facilitators make their contribution by:

- conducting background research to understand the needs of the group and what they hope to achieve
- helping the group define its overall goal, as well as its specific objectives
- preparing a detailed agenda that includes process notes describing how the interaction will unfold
- helping the group create rules of conduct that create an effective climate
- making sure that assumptions are surfaced and tested
- questioning and probing to encourage deeper exploration
- offering the right tools and techniques at the right moment
- encouraging participation by everyone

- guiding group discussion to keep it on track
- making accurate notes that reflect the members' ideas
- helping members constructively manage differences of opinion and redirecting ineffective behaviors
- providing feedback to the group so that it can assess its progress and make adjustments
- helping achieve closure and identify next steps
- helping the group access resources from inside and outside the group
- providing a means for evaluating the meeting and seeking improvements.

Facilitators bring structure to interactions to make them productive. They plan carefully and then adapt as things unfold. For more on how facilitators organize and manage their work, refer to Chapter Three on the stages of the facilitation process.

 Facilitators believe that two heads are better than one.

 A facilitator's job is to manage the process and leave the content to the participants.

Differentiating Between Process and Content

The two words you'll hear over and over again in facilitation are process and content. These are the two dimensions of any interaction between people.

The *content* of any meeting is **what** is being discussed: the task at hand, the subjects being dealt with, and the problems being solved. The content is expressed in the agenda and the words that are spoken. Because it's the verbal portion of the meeting, the content is obvious and typically consumes the attention of the members.

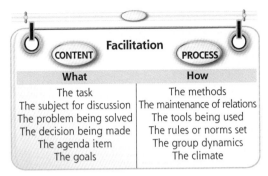

Facilitation	
CONTENT	PROCESS
What	**How**
The task	The methods
The subject for discussion	The maintenance of relations
The problem being solved	The tools being used
The decision being made	The rules or norms set
The agenda item	The group dynamics
The goals	The climate

Process deals with **how** things are being discussed: the methods, procedures, format, and tools used. The process also includes the style of the interaction, the group dynamics, and the climate that's established. Because the process is silent, it's harder to pinpoint. It's the aspect of most meetings that's largely unseen and often ignored, while people are focused on the content.

When the person leading the meeting offers an opinion with the intent of influencing the outcome of discussions, he or she is acting as the "content leader." When a facilitator offers tools and focuses on managing member interaction, he or she is acting as the "process leader."

While facilitators are totally unassertive about the content under discussion, they are very assertive in the way they manage the process elements. This assertiveness is needed to deal with conflict, make interventions, and help the group when it gets stuck.

At first glance, facilitation may seem like a rather vague set of "warm and fuzzy," people-oriented stuff. But as you'll learn, it's actually a highly structured and assertive set of practices with a rich set of tools and techniques. Once you understand these techniques and learn how to apply them, you'll immediately see substantial improvement in the overall performance of any group.

Content vs. Process Leadership

A meeting leader offering an opinion with the intent of influencing the outcome of discussions is acting as a content leader.

In contrast, when a meeting leader is neutral on the content and focuses on managing the proceedings, he or she is acting as the process leader or facilitator. It's the facilitator's job to manage the process.

Facilitation Tools

As a facilitator you'll have an extensive set of tools at your disposal. These tools fall into two categories: the *Core Practices* and the *Process Tools*.

The **Core Practices**, which are rooted in the manner, style, and behavior of the facilitator, include:

Staying Neutral

Listening Actively

Asking Questions

Paraphrasing Continuously

Summarizing Discussions

Recording Ideas

Synthesizing Ideas

Keeping on Track

Testing Assumptions

Managing the Climate

The **Process Tools**, which are structured activities that provide a clear sequence of steps, include:

Visioning Force-Field Analysis

Brainstorming

Priority-Setting Surveys

Root-Cause Analysis

Gap Analysis Decision Grids

Systematic Problem Solving

Understanding each of these tools and how to use them is a vital part of any facilitator's job.

Core Practices Overview

Regardless of the type of meeting they're managing or the specific process tool being used, facilitators make constant use of the following core practices. Of these, the first five are foundational. These are in constant use during facilitation, regardless of what other tools are also deployed.

❗ The core practices are the foundation of the facilitator's style.

1: *Facilitators stay neutral on the content.* Staying neutral on the content of discussions is the hallmark of the facilitator role. Facilitators are neutral outsiders who have no stake in the outcome of discussions. They are there only to provide structure and create a climate of collaborations. When facilitators ask questions or make helpful suggestions, they never do this to impose their views or impact decisions.

2: *They listen actively.* This is listening to understand rather than to judge. It also means using attentive body language and looking participants in the eye while they're speaking. Eye contact can also be used to acknowledge points and prompt quiet people to participate in the discussion.

3: *They ask questions.* Questioning is the most fundamental facilitator tool. Questions can be used to test assumptions, probe for hidden information, challenge assumptions, and ratify for consensus. Effective questioning encourages people to look past symptoms to get at root causes.

4 : *They paraphrase continuously.* Facilitators paraphrase continuously during discussions. Paraphrasing involves repeating what group members say. This lets people know they are heard and acknowledges their input. Paraphrasing also lets others hear points for a second time and provides an opportunity to clarify ideas.

5 : *They summarize discussions.* Facilitators summarize ideas shared by members at the end of every discussion. They do this to ensure that everyone heard all of the ideas that were put forth, to check for accuracy, and to bring closure. Facilitators also summarize in the midst of discussions to arrive at consensus, to catch everyone up on the conversation and to refresh the topic during conversation lulls. Summarizing is useful to restart a stalled discussion, since it reminds group members of the points already made and sparks new thinking. In many decision-making discussions, consensus is created when the facilitator gives the group a clear and concise summary of key points.

In addition to the five techniques described above, there are several additional facilitator techniques that make up the core practices.

Facilitators record ideas. Groups need to leave meetings with complete and accurate notes that summarize discussions. Facilitators quickly and accurately record what's being said. Whether they are using a flip chart or electronic whiteboard, they are careful to use the key words that people suggest and organize the notes into related groupings.

They synthesize ideas. Facilitators ping-pong ideas around the group to ensure that people build on each other's ideas. In non-decision-making conversations they do this to build conversation and create synergy. In decision-making conversations they ping-pong ideas to allow each person to add his or her comments to the points made by others until they have synthesized a statement everyone can live with.

They keep discussions on track. When discussions veer off track or when people lose focus, facilitators notice this and tactfully point it out. They place a Parking Lot sheet on a wall and offer participants the option of placing extraneous topics on it for later discussion.

They test assumptions. Facilitators outline the parameters, empowerment levels, and other constraints that apply so that they are understood by all. They are always on the lookout for situations in which misunderstandings are rooted in differing assumptions and probe carefully to uncover these.

They manage the group climate. Facilitators help members set behavioral norms or group guidelines. Then they intervene tactfully when they notice that members are not adhering to their own rules. (See later chapters for more on both norms and making interventions.)

They make periodic process checks. This involves tactfully stopping the action whenever group effectiveness declines. Facilitators can intervene to check whether the purpose is still clear to everyone, the process is working, and the pace is effective or to see how people are feeling.

They give and receive feedback. Facilitators always have their fingers on the pulse of the group and offer their perspective to help the group make adjustments. They are also receptive to input and invite members to point out anything that needs adjustment. At the end of each meeting, facilitators create mechanisms such as written evaluations or exit surveys to capture feedback for ongoing improvement.

What Does "Neutral" Mean?

Staying neutral is challenging in facilitation. While it's essential to focus on process and stay out of content, there are three techniques that can be used to give direction without compromising your neutral role.

Neither asking questions nor offering suggestions oversteps the boundaries of neutrality.

External parties can more easily remain neutral than leaders or peers.

1st Strategy—Ask Questions For example, if the group is spinning its wheels because it can't afford new computers, the facilitator can ask: *"What are the benefits of renting new computers as an interim strategy?"*

2nd Strategy—Offer Suggestions If the facilitator has a good content idea that the group should consider, it's within the bounds of the neutral role to offer the group a suggestion for consideration. You might say: *"I suggest that you consider researching the pros/cons of renting computers."*

3rd Strategy—Take Off the Facilitator's Hat In these rare cases, it's important for the facilitator to clearly indicate that he or she is stepping out of the role and explain that he or she is now playing a content role. The facilitator might say: *"I need to step out of the role of facilitator for a minute and tell you that the office location you're considering isn't close to any of the rapid transit corridors planned for the future."*

Learn to say "okay" instead of "good point."

Use "we" ("How are we doing on time?") when re-ferring to the process and "you" ("Let me read back what you've said so far") when reviewing content.

How Assertive Can a Facilitator Be?

While it's true that facilitators should be non-directive on the topic being discussed, they have to be assertive on the process aspects of any meeting. It's within the parameters of the facilitator role to decide all aspects of the meeting process, including informing members how agenda items will be handled, which discussion tools will be used, who will speak in which order, and so on.

This doesn't mean that you shouldn't collaborate with members on the session design. Gaining member input enhances buy-in. It does mean that process is the special expertise of the facilitator. In matters of process, it's appropriate for the facilitator to have the final say.

Just how appropriate and necessary a high level of assertiveness is can be best understood when a group becomes dysfunctional. In these situations, facilitators need to be firm and act like referees, stepping into the fray to restore order to the proceedings.

A high level of assertiveness on process is especially critical whenever there are personal attacks or other rude behavior. You are empowered to interrupt and redirect individuals to ensure interactions are appropriate. Follow these practices and you'll behave in a way that's anything but passive. Some assertive actions when warranted:

- ○ insisting on meeting design and norms
- ○ stopping to check the process and summarize discussions
- ○ calling time-outs and breaks
- ○ intervening to stop rude behavior and calling on quiet people
- ○ asking probing questions and challenging assumptions
- ○ insisting on closure and action plans
- ○ implementing evaluation activities

The Language of Facilitation

A specific style of language has evolved that lets facilitators manage interactions without sounding critical or judgmental. The main language techniques are:

- paraphrasing
- reporting behavior
- describing feelings
- checking perception

Paraphrasing involves describing, in your own words, what another person's remarks convey.

> *"Do I understand you correctly that . . ."*
>
> *"Are you saying . . ."*
>
> *"What I'm hearing you say is . . ."*

Facilitators paraphrase continuously, especially if the discussion starts to spin in circles or if the conversation becomes heated. This repetition assures participants that their ideas are being heard.

 Mastering the language of facilitation will help you avoid sounding critical or judgmental.

Reporting behavior consists of stating the specific, observable actions of others without making accusations or generalizations about them as people, or attributing motives to them.

> *"I'm noticing that we've only heard from three people throughout most of this discussion."*
>
> *"I'm noticing that several people are looking through their journals and writing."*

By describing specific behaviors, facilitators give participants information about how their actions are being perceived. Feeding this information back in a non-threatening manner opens the door to improve the existing situation.

 New facilitators often make the mistake of not paraphrasing enough.

Describing feelings consists of specifying or identifying feelings by naming the feeling with a metaphor or a figure of speech.

"I feel we've run out of energy." (naming)

"I feel as if we're facing a brick wall." (metaphor)

"I feel like a fly on the wall." (figure of speech)

Facilitators always need to be honest with group members by saying things like:

"I feel exhausted right now." or

"I feel frustrated."

This lets other people know that it's okay for them to express feelings.

Checking perception is describing another person's inner state in order to check if that perception is correct.

"You appear upset by the last comment that was made. Are you?"

"You seem impatient. Are you anxious to move on to the next topic?"

Perception checking is a very important tool. It lets the facilitator take the pulse of participants who might be experiencing emotions that get in the way of their participation.

Conversation Structures

One of the most important mental models in facilitation is that conversations fall into two distinct categories: They are either decision-making in nature or not. Each type of conversation has distinct features that dictate the techniques used to manage it. Facilitators who understand these two distinct conversation structures can use them to structure and manage discussions.

Non-Decision-Making Conversations

Group members simply share ideas or information. Examples of non-decision-making conversations include:

- a brainstorming session in which ideas are generated but not judged

- an information-sharing session in which members describe their experiences or update each other

- a discussion aimed at making a list of individual preferences or key factors in a situation.

Members state ideas, but there is no element of judging or ranking the ideas. The facilitator simply records ideas as they are presented without the need to check with others to test their views.

 Always know whether you're facilitating a decision-making conversation or one in which no decisions are being made.

Decision-Making Conversations

Group member ideas are combined to arrive at either an action plan or a rule that all members must feel they can implement or accept.

Facilitators need to manage decision-making conversations differently because they need to help members arrive at a shared agreement. This involves clarifying ideas, ping-ponging ideas around so others can add their thoughts, making statements that summarize the discussion, and recording the group opinion.

In non-decision-making conversations facilitators record what individuals think. In decision-making conversations they record what the group thinks. In summary:

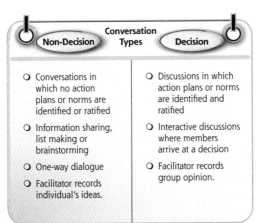

Conversation Types

Non-Decision

- Conversations in which no action plans or norms are identified or ratified
- Information sharing, list making or brainstorming
- One-way dialogue
- Facilitator records individual's ideas.

Decision

- Discussions in which action plans or norms are identified and ratified
- Interactive discussions where members arrive at a decision
- Facilitator records group opinion.

Starting a Facilitation

Start Sequences have three components:

1. **The Purpose**—A statement that clearly describes the goal of the facilitated discussion. This is what will be discussed. A simple goal statement or a more detailed description of the desired outcomes.

2. **The Process**—A statement of how the session will be conducted. This helps the participants understand how decisions will be made, the speaking order, and any structuring tools that will be used. It also clarifies if members are contributing input or making final decisions.

3. **The Timeframe**—A statement of how long the entire discussion will take. In more complex conversations, timeframes should also be provided for segments.

Start Sequence Variations

Start Sequences can be simple or complex and created ahead of time, by getting input from group members and then feeding that input back at the beginning of a discussion. In other situations the Start Sequence is created at the start of a discussion. In these instances the facilitator can invite group members to make a statement about the purpose of the session and then test that statement with everyone to ensure a shared understanding.

While group member input is almost always sought to define the purpose, facilitators usually provide the process. Describing the process is important because it helps the participants understand how the topic will be managed.

Clearly defining the timeframe for a specific discussion is always a good idea. One of the biggest problems in meetings is that they can drag on. By engaging members in a discussion about time, the facilitator can help members set boundaries. Once members have agreed to timeframes, it's also easier for the facilitator to intervene if agreed-upon timeframes are being violated.

Facilitation at a Glance! | Fourth Edition | ©2018 GOAL/QPC

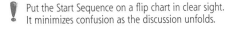

> Put the Start Sequence on a flip chart in clear sight. It minimizes confusion as the discussion unfolds.

Start Sequence Examples

A Simple Start Sequence: *Time: 25 minutes.*

Purpose: To make recommendations to the committee empowered to renovate staff common areas.

Process: Brainstorming of ideas by the large group. Multi-voting to rank the ideas.

A Complex Start Sequence:

Purpose: To discuss the recent new product launch campaign in order to identify the lessons learned. To leave with a clear list of the things that we did well, the things that we did not execute well, and specific strategies for overcoming the things that we did not execute effectively to improve our next launch.

Process steps:

1: In a large group, identify all of the things that went well and the contributing factors at every step of the launch. Tell success stories to celebrate the positives and isolate what made each element work.

2: Have group members individually write all the things that did not go well at each launch stage on index cards and place them on the walls.

3: Hold a plenary to read all the posted issues aloud.

4: Use multi-voting to rank the execution issues.

5: Break into small groups to apply the steps of systematic problem solving to the four top-ranked items.

6: Hold a plenary to hear the top-ranked recommendations for action from each team and ratify these in the large group.

Learn to differentiate between simple and complex Start Sequences.

Timeframe: (1) 35 min, (2) 40 min, (3) 30 min, (4) 30 min (with break), (5) 60 min, (6) 45 min.

Total = 240 minutes or 4 hours.

During a Facilitation

Once a discussion is underway, it can easily get side-tracked or stuck, even when there's a clear Start Sequence in place. A few reasons why:

- the topic may be more complex than anticipated
- the conversation may have drifted onto another topic
- the process tool being used may not be the right one
- the original timeframes may not have been realistic
- individuals may be feeling tired or lose focus.

Sometimes there are obvious signs that these things have happened, but there are also lots of times when there are no outward signs that meeting effectiveness is declining. It's vital that facilitators periodically stop the action and conduct a process check.

A process check is a type of intervention designed to test effectiveness even when there are no outward signs of problems. As with all interventions, the sole purpose is to restore the effectiveness of the group.

Conducting a process check involves stopping the action to shift member focus to the process or how things are going.

Process-Checking Structure

There are four basic areas of inquiry in process checking. Facilitators can check just one element, two, three, or all four.

1. Progress
2. Process
3. Pace
4. People

 Make it a routine to conduct process checks, even when there are no signs of problems.

1. Progress: Ask the members if they think the goal of the meeting is being achieved. Do they think that the purpose is still clear? Do they think that the discussion is still on topic? Do they feel that they're making progress?

When to check the progress: If few ideas are emerging, when the conversation goes in circles, at periodic intervals, or at points of closure.

2. Process: Ask members whether they feel that the tool or approach being used is working. Ask whether any progress is being made using this approach. Ask how much longer they're willing to keep using that approach. Offer other tools.

When to check the process: When the tool being used isn't yielding results, when it's evident that the designated process isn't being followed, or at periodic intervals.

3. Pace: Ask members if things are moving at the right pace.

When to check the pace: When timelines are not being met or at periodic intervals.

4. People: Ask people how they are feeling. Ask whether anyone has lost the thread of the conversation.

When to check the people: When the meeting has been going on for a while, when people grow silent and withdraw, or when people look tired or frustrated.

Why Process Checks Are Important

Process checks are like an early warning system that lets the facilitator detect problems while there's still time to take corrective action. This avoids the pitfall of finding out at the end of a meeting that things had been off track since the early stages.

Ending a Facilitation

One of the biggest meeting pitfalls is ending without real closure or detailed next steps. When members leave a meeting without action plans, the entire meeting can feel like a waste of time.

 It's essential to bring proper closure to all discussions.

Whether ending a short discussion or an extended meeting, facilitators always provide a summary of key points to ensure that there's a shared view of the outcome.

Even if the session was a non-decision-making session, facilitators should provide a concise summary of what was discussed.

Ending a Non-Decision-Making Session

At the end of a discussion during which people shared information, brainstormed ideas, or made lists, it's a facilitator best practice to provide a summary of the points discussed. This allows people to add any points that were missed and it brings closure.

Ending a Decision-Making Session

At the end of a session during which group members made one or more decisions, the facilitator needs to not only recap what was decided, but also ratify the outcome and ensure that clear action steps are in place. This can include:

- reviewing the details of the decision(s)
- checking the decision(s) for clarity and completeness
- ratifying the decision by asking each member whether he or she can live with the outcome to reduce the risks of post-meeting loss of commitment
- identifying of next steps and creating detailed action plans
- troubleshooting the action plan by asking and answering questions like:

"What sudden shifts could change priorities or block implementation?"

In addition to helping group members summarize and plan for action, facilitators also do some or all of the following to end a facilitation:

- round up parking lot items and help members identify how to deal with them in the future
- help members create an agenda for the next meeting
- decide on a means of follow-up: either written reports, emails, or personal report-back sessions
- help members decide who will transcribe the flip chart sheets
- allow group members to take digital snapshots of flip charts if they have an immediate need for notes
- help members evaluate the session
- thank group members for the privilege of facilitating.

 It's essential to record member ideas on an electronic or paper flip chart so everyone can see the progress being made.

The Rules of Wording

Since facilitators always strive to be neutral to ensure that group members control outcomes. It's important to accurately record what people say without editing too much. If the facilitator changes too many words or adds words that he or she personally prefers, group members will feel that the facilitator has taken control of the proceedings. The first rule of recording ideas is, therefore, to **faithfully record what people are saying.**

Since people say much more than we can record in a few crisp statements, facilitators are always challenged to create a short, concise summary of the dialogue.

Rule 1

Use their words—Listen carefully for the key words that participants use and ensure that these words are included in what is written on the flip chart. For example:

> *"I'm writing the word 'disaster' because you emphasized it."*

> *"Let me read you back what I wrote to check whether I accurately captured your point."*

 If you don't understand a point or momentarily lose focus, recap!

Rule 2

Ask permission to change words—If participants struggle to articulate a point, offer wording, but get member approval to ensure that what's recorded reflects what's intended.

> *"I've shortened what you said to this. . . Is this okay?"*

> *"Can I use the word. . .?"*

> *"Is it okay to record that this way?"*

> *"Tell me what you want me to write down."*

> *"Give me the exact words you need to see on the page."*

DO	**Flip Chart Management**	**DON'T**

DO	**DON'T**
Write down exactly what's said. While comments have to be edited somewhat, always use their key words. Check to make sure that what's written captures the meaning expressed.	Write down your personal interpretation of things– These are their notes. If unsure, ask, *"What should I write down?"*
Use verbs and make phrases fairly complete. For example, writing "work group" is not as helpful as writing "work group to meet Mon. at 10 a.m." Always be sure the flip chart can convey meaning, even to absentees.	Worry about spelling–If you make a fuss, it will inhibit members from getting up and taking a turn at facilitating.
Talk and write at the same time. This helps maintain a good pace.	Hide behind the flip chart or talk to it–Stand beside it.
Move around and act alive. Don't act as though you're chained to the flip chart. If an important point is being made, walk closer to the person who is talking so you can pay attention.	Stand passively at the flip chart without writing anything down–Make note of key words and ideas, comprehensive statements can be formulated later.
Write in black, blue, or some other dark color. Use fairly large letters so it can be read from the back of the room.	Use script unless you have great handwriting, red and pale pastels can be difficult to see from any distance.
Post flip sheets around the room so that people can keep track of what has been discussed.	Monopolize the flip chart.
Whenever appropriate, let others take over both large-and small-group facilitation. This builds commitment and reinforces the idea that this isn't the facilitator's meeting.	Monopolize managing the meeting process.

Best and Worst Facilitation Practices

Some of the best things a facilitator can do:

BEST

- o carefully assess the needs of the members

- o probe sensitively into people's feelings

- o create an open and trusting atmosphere

- o help people understand why they're there

- o view yourself as serving the group's needs

- o make members the center of attention

- o speak in simple and direct language

- o work hard to stay neutral

- o display energy and appropriate levels of assertiveness

- o champion ideas you don't personally favor

- o treat all participants as equals

- o stay flexible and ready to change direction if necessary

- o listen intently to fully understand what's being said

- o make notes that reflect what participants mean

- o periodically summarize related ideas into a coherent summary

- o know how to use a wide range of process tools

- o make sure every session ends with clear steps for the next meeting

- o ensure that participants feel ownership for what has been achieved

- o end on a positive and optimistic note

Some of the worst things a facilitator can do:

- remain oblivious to what the group thinks or needs
- never check member concerns
- fail to listen carefully to what's being said
- lose track of key ideas
- take poor notes or change the meaning of what's said

- try to be the center of attention
- get defensive
- get into personality battles
- put people down
- avoid or ignore conflict
- let a few people or the leader dominate
- never check how the meeting is going
- be overly passive on process
- push ahead on an irrelevant agenda
- have no alternative approaches
- let discussions get badly sidetracked
- let discussions ramble without proper closure
- be oblivious about when to stop
- be insensitive to cultural diversity issues
- use inappropriate humor

Facilitator Behaviors and Strategies

Regardless of whether you're a facilitator from within the group or from outside, or whether you are the team's leader or a member, the following are parameters for facilitator behaviors.

Be informed—Successful facilitators always gather extensive data about their prospective participants in order to fully understand both their business and their needs. They survey and interview participants, read background reports, and use prepared questions to build a complete picture of the group's situation.

Be optimistic—Facilitators don't let disinterest, antagonism, shyness, cynicism, or other negative reactions throw them off. Instead, they focus on what can be achieved and strategies to draw the best from each participant.

Be consensual—Facilitation is fundamentally a consensus-building process. Facilitators always strive to create outcomes that reflect the ideas of all participants equally.

Be flexible—Successful facilitators always have a process plan for all meetings, yet at the same time are always ready to toss it aside and change direction if that's what is needed. Really great facilitators possess a wide repertoire of process tools and come prepared with alternative strategies.

Be understanding—Facilitators need to understand that there are great pressures on employees in today's workplace and that antagonistic or cynical behaviors may be a result of high stress levels.

Be alert—Accomplished facilitators are expert people watchers. They pay careful attention to group dynamics and notice what's going on at all times.

They are attuned to noticing both how people interact and how well they're achieving the task.

Be firm—Good facilitation is not a passive activity, but one that calls for substantial assertiveness. Facilitators should always be ready to step in and redirect an ineffective process.

Be unobtrusive—The facilitator should do as little talking as possible. The participants should be doing all of the talking. The facilitator says only enough to give instructions, stop arguments, keep things on track, and sum up. Trying to be the center of attention or make yourself look important is a misuse of your position.

> **!** Facilitating should be an egoless activity. The purpose is to make the group succeed, not to make yourself look really important and clever. An effective facilitator will leave a group convinced that "We did it ourselves."

Success

Facilitation Checklist

Start	❏ Welcome participants ❏ Introduce members ❏ Explain your role ❏ Clarify session goal ❏ Explain the process ❏ Set time frames ❏ Appoint time keepers ❏ Create parking lot ❏ Start the discussion	**Remember** Stay neutral Listen actively Ask questions Paraphrase continuously Provide summaries Record ideas Synthesize ideas Keep on track
During	❏ Check the purpose ❏ Check the process ❏ Check the pace ❏ Test assumptions ❏ Maintain the climate	**Manage Conflict** 1. Vent concerns and feelings 2. Solve problems

End	❏ Summarize discussions
	❏ Clarify and ratify
	  decisions
	❏ Create action plans
	❏ Force-field analysis
	❏ Round up leftover
	  items
	❏ Help create next
	  agenda
	❏ Clarify follow-up
	  process
	❏ Evaluate the session
		Utilize Toolkit
		Visioning
		S.W.A.T/S.O.A.R.
		Brainstorming
		5 Whys
		Force-field
		Needs and offers
		Multi-voting
		Gap analysis
		Root-cause analysis
		Decision grids
		Problem solving

Facilitator Behaviors

HELP	HINDER
__ listens actively	__ is oblivious to group needs
__ maintains eye contact	__ no follow-up on concerns
__ helps identify needs	__ poor listening
__ gets buy-in	__ strays into content
__ surfaces concerns	__ loses track of key ideas
__ defines problems	__ makes poor notes
__ brings everyone into discussion	__ ignores conflicts
__ uses good body language	__ provides no alternatives for
__ paraphrases continuously	structuring the discussion
__ accepts and uses feedback	__ gets defensive
__ checks time and pace	__ doesn't paraphrase enough
__ provides useful feedback	__ lets a few people dominate
__ monitors and adjusts the process	__ never checks how it's going
__ asks relevant, probing questions	__ is the center of attention
__ keeps an open attitude	__ lets the group get sidetracked
__ stays neutral	__ projects a poor image
__ offers helpful suggestions	__ uses negative or sarcastic tone
__ is optimistic and positive	__ talks too much
__ manages conflict well	__ puts people down
__ takes a problem-solving approach	__ doesn't know when to stop
__ stays focused on process	
__ ping-pongs ideas around	**Additional Observations:**
__ makes accurate notes that reflect	
the discussion	
__ effectively uses humor	
__ looks calm and pleasant	
__ is flexible about changing the	
approach used	
__ skillfully summarizes what is said	
__ knows when to stop	

Facilitation Skill Levels

Mastering the art of neutrality, keeping notes, and asking questions at meetings is a start. Being a true facilitator means developing your competency at four distinct levels.

Review the skills needed at each level to zero in on your current strengths and to identify those areas where you may wish to enhance your current skills.

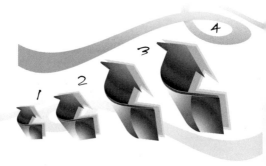

Level *1*—Understanding concepts, values, and beliefs; using facilitative behaviors such as active listening, paraphrasing, questioning, and summarizing; managing time; encouraging participation; keeping clear and accurate notes; using basic tools like problem solving and action planning.

Level *2*—Mastering process tools; designing meetings; skilled at using the right decision-making method, achieving consensus, and getting true closure; handling feedback activities and conducting process checks; using exit surveys; good at managing meetings in an effective manner; able to help a group set goals and objectives that are measurable; skilled at checking assumptions and challenging ideas.

Level 3—Skilled at managing conflict and making immediate interventions; able to deal with resistance and personal attacks; making design changes on the spot; sizing up a group and using the right strategies for its developmental stage; managing survey feedback exercises; able to design and conduct interviews and focus groups; designing and implementing surveys; consolidating ideas from a mass of information into coherent summaries.

Level 4—Designing and implementing process interventions in response to complex organizational issues; using tools to promote process improvement, customer intimacy, and overall organizational effectiveness; able to support teams in the various stages of team development.

FACILITATORS
ACT A LOT
LIKE REFEREES
WHO BRING
STRUCTURE AND
ORDER WITHOUT
INTERFERING
WITH THE
ACTION.

TWO

EFFECTIVE QUESTIONING

Questions are the heart and soul of facilitation. Facilitation is, after all, about asking for input instead of telling people what to do. Questions are the main technique for getting people to open up, reflect, imagine, buy-in, identify problems and discover creative solutions.

It's important to understand that there's a lot more to questioning than simply asking the first thing that pops into your head. Questions have structure and need to be carefully designed to ensure that they're sensitive and on target. That's why professional facilitators carefully plan the questions they're going to ask. Planning ensures that they're asking the right question, the right way, at the right time.

To zero in on the right question to pose in a particular situation ask yourself the following three questions:

What do I want to ask? What information is needed to create a clear and comprehensive picture of the group's situation? What background, facts, opinions, feeling, reflections and suggestions do I need to pull from the group.

Why do I want to ask this? What are my motives for asking specific questions? Am I trying to find out about the group's problems, the objectives of key group members, lingering feeling about past change, and so forth?

2 | Effective Questioning

How might people respond? How might group members respond? Could there be defensiveness, anger or even fear associated with asking specific questions? What reactions am I trying to provoke? What reactions do I want to avoid?

Understanding your aims in pursuing a line of questioning will help to ensure that those questions are on target.

The Principles of Effective Questioning

One of the great challenges of questioning effectively is that there isn't a standard set of questions that works in every setting. A line of questioning that works really well with one group might confuse or upset another one. Even the questions contained in this chapter are only offered as food for thought. It's always important to evaluate every question to ensure that it's appropriate.

Keep these guidelines in mind:

1: **Customize for context:** Be sure that questions are sensitive to things like the client's organizational culture, occupational group, gender mix, values, environmental factors, financial situation, recent history and current stresses.

2: **Create inviting questions:** Avoid embedding too many of your own thoughts and suggestions inside questions. This will lead people to answers that you favor and will make you look manipulative. Ask the kind of open-ended questions that encourage deep, creative thought.

3: **Ask with sensitivity:** Unless you decide to deliberately confront your clients to shake them out of complacent thinking, questions should always be asked mindfully. That means avoiding harsh language and verbal traps that raise client anxiety and increase distrust. Maintaining positive body language is a big part of this too.

4: Clarify assumptions: Check out your understanding of what clients are saying. Sometimes they use language differently or understate how they really feel. Ask things like: "Am I correct in thinking that...". "Let me see if I've understood correctly that..." or "Are you saying that...".

Question Types

There are two basic question types: closed-ended and open-ended. Each has its uses, but facilitators predominantly use open-ended questions because they encourage clients to engage.

	Question Types	
Type of Question	**Description**	**Example**
Closed-ended	Elicits one-word answers and tends to close discussion	"Does everyone understand the changes we've discussed?"
	Solicits yes/no answers or ratings	"Where is this on a scale of 1-5, with 5 being excellent?
	Useful to clarify and test assumptions	"Have I given a clear description of the situation?"
	Often begins with "is," "can," "how many," or "does"	"Does any of this need more elaboration?"
Open-ended	Requires more than yes/no answers	"What ideas do you have for explaining the changes to our customer?"
	Stimulates thinking. Often begins with "what," "how," "when," or "why"	"If we were going to do something totally innovative, what would that look like?"

Questioning Formats

The sample questions in this chapter are organized according to their intention. In addition, each question also represents one of the following questioning formats. You can use these various questioning structures to ensure that your facilitation work evokes a broad range of responses. Facilitators are always careful not to get in the rut of relying on just one type of question.

Fact-finding questions are targeted at verifiable data such as who, what, when, where and how much. Use them to gather information about the current situation.

> *"What kind of computer equipment are you using now?"*

> *"How much training did staff receive at the start of the project?"*

Feeling-finding questions ask for subjective information that gets at the participants' opinions, feelings, values and beliefs. They help you understand gut reactions.

> *"How do you feel about the new office layout?"*

> *"What kind of reaction are you expecting from the staff?"*

Tell-me-more questions encourage people to provide more details. They encourage people to elaborate.

> *"Tell me more."*

> *"Can you elaborate on that?"*

> *"What else comes to mind?"*

Best/worst questions help you understand potential opportunities in the present situation. They let you test for the outer limits of participants' wants and needs.

> *"What's the best thing about switching software?"*

> *"What's the worst thing about installing new software?"*

Third-party questions help uncover thoughts in an indirect manner. They allow people to speculate on what others might think, without challenging them to reveal their personal thoughts.

"Do you have any thoughts about why some people might resist this idea?"

"Why would a team member not want to attend a team-building session?"

Magic wand questions let you explore people's desires. Also known as crystal ball questions, these are useful to temporarily remove obstacles from a person's mind.

"If money were no object, which software would you buy?"

"If you had total control over the project, what would you change?"

The Importance of Follow-on Questions

One of the most important aspects of effective questioning is the ability to ask the right follow-on questions. Follow-on questioning matters because the initial reply to a question often fails to get to the underlying issue. Think of follow-on questioning as *"peeling the onion"* to get to the heart of what's really going on. Some lines of questioning may need to be pursued three or four times to get to the core issue.

While the exact wording of follow-on questions can't be predicted, there are some general principles to keep in mind:

1. Start with straightforward fact-finding questions.

2. Follow up with questions that clarify the initial responses.

3. Ask for the rationale behind these responses.

4. Ask how things unfolded.

5. Use feeling-finding questions to get at the emotions buried at the core of the matter.

6. Use third-party or magic wand questions if people seem blocked.

Asking Sensitive Questions

Other than those rare instances when a group needs to be deliberately confronted in order to avoid a catastrophe, facilitators work hard to avoid anything that feels threatening. When a line of questioning touches on a sensitive topic, facilitators often allow people to write their responses on pieces of paper. These are collected and tabulated before being shared, to ensure group member safety. This is especially true when questions press people to disclose information of a personal nature.

Here are some ways to safely ask tough questions:

- Create an anonymous way to gather data. This can be a paper survey that respondents return in a sealed envelope, a reply that they send via email to your office only, or an anonymous reply on an automated survey form.

- Use slips of paper. Allow a few minutes for quiet reflection and writing. Have people pass their notes to you. Mix them up and read them aloud without reference to who made which comment.

- Pose sensitive questions with a 1-5 rating scale on a flip chart or whiteboard. Invite people to write their rating on a slip of paper, collect these and post the ratings. No one will know who gave which scores.

- Place a question and rating scale on a flip chart. Allow time for people to write their score on a slip of paper. Turn the flip chart toward a corner and invite people to file by one at a time to post their answers. Brave people will go first, while those who feel most nervous will wait to post their ratings after there are several numbers already on the board. Turn the board around to share the ratings.

The Question Bank

On the following pages you'll find samples of questions facilitators routinely ask. To make them more relevant, they've been reframed to fit a third party context. The best way to use these sample questions is to think of them as food for thought.

Many of the sample questions can be used "off the shelf," but most will be more effective if they're adapted to fit the context. While most questions are asked in the moment, note that it's often a good idea to send questions to group members in advance so that they have time to reflect and prepare appropriate answers. These questions can be used in groups, on surveys and one-to-one.

Questions to Get to Know a New Client

"Tell me the story of the organization."

"What would you say was the organization's outstanding strength/achievement?"

"What's the organization's image with the public?

"What values drive this organization?"

"Is your organization culture generally receptive to outside input and to making major change?"

"Does the organization work through departmental silos or do people work cross-functionally?"

"When a change is being contemplated, does management deliberately seek out employee input?'

"Does the organization have a peer feedback or upward feedback process?"

"What would your most satisfied customers say about you?"

"What words would your main competitors use to describe you?"

"Is there anything about the organization that an outsider like me might find confusing/surprising?"

"What have been the organization's major turning points/ challenges and how were they handled?"

"Who has been most instrumental in making the organization a success?"

"What role have you played in that success?"

"What would you guess were the things that the people who work here are most proud of?"

"What's the greatest strength of the people inside this company?"

"If you had a magic wand, what one thing would you change immediately?"

"If you could turn back the hands of time, what one event would you go back and change?"

"Rate the current organizational state on a scale of 1-10, with 10 representing an ideal state."

"Imagine that it's exactly ten years from today and there's a really positive headline in the newspaper about this organization. What does that headline say?"

Questions to Clarify the Consultant-Client Relationship

"Tell me about your past experience with external consultants. How might those experiences affect our work?"

"What's the number one skill or talent that you're hoping I bring to the project? What are the second and third?"

"What's the best contribution that I can make to this project?"

"Describe your idea of the ideal consultant/client relationship?"

"What powers do you think I will need to be able manage the various challenges that could crop up?"

"Who should I be talking to on a regular basis? Are there any parties I shouldn't communicate with directly?"

Questions to Help People Get to Know One Another

"If you had to condense your resume down to four sentences, what would they be?"

"Give us a single snapshot from your youth that tells us who you are today."

"Where are you from? Tell us one interesting thing about your hometown/ youth/ college years?"

"Tell us the three main things/events/talents that got you to where you are today?"

"Complete this sentence: My ultimate career destiny is to…?"

"What's the hidden talent, past experience or hobby most people here don't know about you?"

"What's the most enjoyable part of your job?"

"What part of your current job do you find most challenging?"

"If you had to name one additional skill or bit of education you'd like to acquire, what would it be?"

"What unique gift, experience or skill do you bring to this organization/project/ team?"

"What would your colleagues say was your main contribution to the workplace?"

"What motivates you to do a great job?"

"What traits do you most need to see in a leader? In a team member?"

"If you could invite three thoughtful people or leaders in your field to be part of this team, whom would you ask and why?"

Questions to Assess the Current Situation

"What are the things that this organization does exceedingly well?"

"What are the things that this organization does just okay?"

"What are the things that this organization does poorly?"

"What's going on in the environment that this organization needs to be especially aware of? What about competitors, suppliers, customers, finances, materials, human resources, machinery, etc.?"

"Does the organization have a systematic way of evaluating effectiveness, such as an organized process-improvement program?"

"What are the current barriers to working effectively that we need to pay attention to? Are there communication barriers? Is it difficult to access resources/get approvals, etc.?"

"Given the current situation, what are all the possible approaches you suspect organizational change experts might recommend?"

"What are the consequences for the organization if this project fails?"

"What would be the best possible outcome of this project?"

"If you had to give me one piece of helpful advice, what would it be?"

Questions to Establish Project Parameters

"What are some of the guidelines you've worked with in other projects that you think we should also adopt?"

"Do all projects undergo an initial cost/benefit analysis?"

"How will we make decisions? Who can decide what?"

"Which types of decisions need to be a consensus?"

"How should we communicate about work in progress, problems and issues?"

"How do we avoid starting a rumor mill about possible changes?"

"What are the guidelines about who can talk to whom about what?"

"What's the approval process for missing a deadline or overshooting the budget?"

"How can we always ensure that resources are fairly allocated? What's the process if this doesn't happen?"

"Let's define what we're going to consider a crisis and then decide the best way to handle them."

"How often do I need to report? What form should my reports take?"

"What should we consider to be an emergency? What subroutines should we establish to ensure that these are handled effectively?"

Questions to Establish Behavioral Norms or Rules of Conduct

"Think back to a time when you worked on a team where everybody got along. What attitudes and behaviors did people exhibit? What rules did they follow?"

"What one helpful thing have you learned working on other projects and teams that you think this group should consider making a guideline for this project?"

"List the top five things that motivate you in terms of how you're treated by both leaders and colleagues. Which of these need to become part of how this team operates?"

"What's the best way to head off or avoid interpersonal conflicts or disputes?"

"What kinds of information can we share and what information needs to stay inside the group?"

"Who can receive which types of information?"

"What can we do to ensure that confidentiality is maintained with respect to sensitive information?"

"What should the rule be about people missing project meetings?"

"How should we handle the good times we might encounter as a team? How about the bad times?"

"Under what conditions would you be willing to give and receive feedback about both team and personal performance?"

Questions to Identify Expectations

"Imagine that today is the last meeting of this project and that it was successful beyond your wildest dreams! What would we be celebrating today?"

"In your own words answer the question, 'Why are we here?' "

"What's the burning question that absolutely must be addressed in this project?"

"What are the specific deliverables that need to be accomplished? By what dates?"

"If we asked employees for their hopes for this project, what would they say?"

"If we asked your competition what they would most like to see come out of this project, what would they say?"

"If we could get only two positive outcomes from this entire initiative, what would they be?"

"What do you think employees are hoping to gain from the changes that will come out of this project?"

"What are the important milestones on the way to a successful outcome?"

"Describe the most positive thing you could personally gain from this project."

"How will we know if we've been successful or unsuccessful?"

Questions to Uncover Issues or Problems

"Describe the biggest problem that this project could encounter, as a one-line newspaper headline."

"If we encounter scope creep, where is this most likely to occur?"

"Could we potentially encounter any ethical issues during this project? What are they?"

"What catastrophic event could cause this project to lose its funding or lose management support?"

"Is there anyone or any group that might benefit from our failure to complete this project?"

"Name a factor outside of our control that could adversely affect the project?"

"On a scale of 1-5, with 1 being none and 5 being lots, how tolerant is the organization of risk in this area?"

"If you had to rank the top three issues being encountered in order of priority, what would they be?"

"How can we improve our capacity to notice issues and deal with them quickly?"

"Are there any recurring patterns in relation to this issue?"

"Are we looking at the whole picture or are we seeing just one small part of something larger?"

"Can you describe fully what's happening with respect to this issue?"

"As an important member of this project, what keeps you awake at night?"

"Are there areas within the organization where commitment or capacity might be a concern?

"What resources can we draw on in times of trouble? How can we build bridges to these resources now? Whom do we need to call on for each type of problem we might encounter?"

Questions to Encourage Creative Thinking

"How would other cultures approach this challenge? What would the Japanese do? The Germans? The Swedes?"

"If we think revolution instead of evolution, how does that change things?"

"If we set out to delight customers instead of just meet their needs, what would that look like?"

"What other companies have totally transformed themselves? What did they do?

"What external resources can the people inside this organization call on?"

"What questions haven't we asked ourselves?"

"Describe some of the most innovative products or approaches to service that you know of. What makes them special?"

"What's the most obvious solution? What's the least obvious?"

"What would we do if money were no object?"

"What would your biggest competitors want you to do?"

"What's the opposite of what we plan to do?" Is there an element of that that we need to consider?"

"What have you never done before that we ought to put on the table?"

"What would an 8-year-old say? What would an 80-year-old say?"

Questions to Assess Resistance to Change

"What are the biggest challenges inherent in our strategy? What stands in our way?"

"What are the biggest external threats that could crop up and hinder our efforts?"

"What is it that people argue most about inside this organization?"

"Is there an aspect of this organization's culture that could factor in blocking change?"

"What is it that most frustrates the people working inside this company?"

"What types of changes do people typically resist? Which of these are we most likely to encounter?"

"Think back to a big project that you worked on before. What roadblocks did you run into?"

"How do you think employees are going to react to this change on a purely gut level?"

Complete this sentence: "The thing that could come out of left field and blindside us is… "

"Who are some of the key players and how might they each react to change?"

"If people are going to resist our recommendations, who's most likely to do that and what form will the resistance take?"

"What are all the factors that we need to consider that might have an impact on successful implementation?"

Questions to Identify Implications

"Let's look at the main ideas on the table and drill down to identify the impacts of each on the project and the organization."

"If we go ahead as planned, what are the expected outcomes? What are some of the potential unintended things we could encounter?"

"What are the potential impacts of downsizing/scaling up/adding a new product/ moving to a new location?

"Look into a crystal ball and tell me what you see that could be an unexpected implication."

"What's one thing we know for sure about the bottom line on this matter?"

Questions to Build Ownership and Commitment

"What is the biggest potential gain for the company? For you personally?"

"What do you personally hope to contribute to this initiative?"

"What will ensure that every single employee gets on board to help make change a reality?"

"What do you feel is the biggest hope that individual employees have with respect to this change?"

"What's the most important factor for getting senior management solidly on our team?"

"What outcome will most ensure that your strategic business partners continue their commitment to you?"

Questions to Prompt for Clarity

"Could you be more specific?"

"Can you say that another way?"

"Please say a little more about that."

"Can you give us another example?"

"What's the opposite of that?"

"Could someone please restate that idea to make sure we all understand this the same way?"

"Tell us all more. How does this impact us?"

Questions to Gain Perspective

"Has anyone experienced a similar situation?"

"What assumptions are we making about this idea?"

"What are the pros and cons of this idea?"

"If we've forgotten one thing, what is it?"

"If this team had a blind spot, what would it be?"

"How might other stakeholders see this issue?"

"How are employees/customers going to react?"

"Let's think of just one more perspective on this so that we can capture another point of view."

"Does anyone have something totally different to suggest?"

Questions to Challenge and Confront

"In what way is our current strategy basically what you've always done?"

"If you had to identify one reason that this project hasn't gone as far as it should or been as bold as it needed to be, what would that be?"

"If there was one human trait that's holding this project back, what would you say it was?"

"How could our actions potentially get in the way of follow-through on change plans?"

"How does the organization contribute to the problem? How do we?

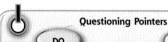

Questioning Pointers

DO	DON'T
Ask clear, concise questions covering a single issue.	Ask rambling, ambiguous questions that cover multiple issues.
Ask a good combination of questions.	Get stuck asking only fact-finding questions.
Retool questions to fit the context.	Ask every client the same questions.
Ask challenging questions that will stimulate thought.	Ask questions without providing an opportunity for thought.
Use mostly open-ended questions.	Forget that closed-ended questions can be useful for testing understanding.
Ask questions that are sensitive to feelings.	Ask trick questions designed to entrap or fool people.
Ask reasonable questions based on what people know.	Ask questions that most people can't answer.
Ask honest and relevant questions.	Ask questions that lead people to the answer you want.
Ask appropriate follow-on questions to get to the heart of the matter.	Assume that the first answer people offer is the only facet of the issue.

Facilitation at a Glance! | Fourth Edition | ©2018 GOAL/QPC

THREE

FACILITATION STAGES

One of the biggest mistakes a facilitator can make is to come to a meeting without assessing the needs of the group or preparing design notes for the session. Before facilitating any meeting, be aware of the specific stages involved to ensure proper planning and implementation.

Stages in Conducting a Facilitation

1. Assessment and Design
2. Feedback and Refinement
3. Final Preparation
4. Starting a Facilitation
5. During a Facilitation
6. Ending a Facilitation
7. Following-up on a Facilitation

While thorough preparation is absolutely essential, experienced facilitators will tell you that most agendas rarely run exactly as planned. Some discussions will inevitably take longer than planned or it may become evident that agenda items need to be addressed in a different order. Any number of things can result in the need to adjust the design mid-stream. In fact, making adjustments on the fly is an art that all facilitators need to master.

1. Assessment and Design

Make sure the meeting design is based on sufficient and adequate information. If you're coming from outside, ask the group's leader to send a letter to all members, informing them that an external facilitator has been hired and that you will be contacting them to gather background information for the agenda.

Start by interviewing the person who asked you to facilitate the meeting. However, don't stop there and assume that this person is necessarily aware of all the needs and interests of the rest of the group. If you also gather information from a cross-section of group members, you will be able to build a more complete picture of the situation, as well as check out the key assumptions.

There's nothing worse than basing the design of a meeting on what one person has told you, only to find that no one else in the group agrees with that assessment!

To assess the needs and status of the group, you can use one or more of the following techniques:

- o   one-on-one interviews
- o   group interviews
- o   surveys
- o   direct observation

Any time you gather data about a group, a summary of that information must always be fed back to the members. This can be done by providing the members with a written summary of the assessment notes or by writing key points on a flip chart and reviewing them briefly at the start of the session.

 Ensure that the members understand and ratify the meeting design.

Facilitators also review any data they collected at the start of the facilitation to help everyone understand how the final agenda was created. If you've done a good job of interpreting the input of group members, the design of the meeting should sound as if it flows directly from the information gathered.

Once background information has been collected and tabulated, and you feel confident that you understand the group's needs, you can create a preliminary design. This includes identifying the objectives of the session and writing an agenda with detailed process notes.

2. Feedback and Refinement

Once you've created a proposed agenda, share the design to gain the group's approval. If your design is intended for a large group or a complex event, such as a planning retreat, this feedback activity will need to be more formal. It's common to meet with a representative sub-group of members so that they can hear the feedback from the data-gathering and review the proposed design being presented. If the design is for a smaller, less complex meeting, it may suffice to discuss your agenda ideas with the leader and/or representative members.

If a disagreement about the design arises, you need to ensure that all viewpoints are heard and that alternate designs are considered. If the group has valid reasons for not wanting to do an exercise (too sensitive to discuss, or objectives have changed, etc.), respect that concern.

On the other hand, you should stand firm and assertively promote your design, especially if meeting members are reluctant to use participatory techniques or have a history of dysfunction. In these cases, listen to their objections, then help them understand your recommendations. Sometimes what they want is not what they need.

Once agreement on a final workshop design has been reached, you can write a brief summary of both the feedback and final version of the design and send it to the group's representatives. This written memorandum will help reduce the potential for misunderstanding.

3. Final Preparation

Professional facilitators spend as much time preparing for a facilitation session as they do leading the actual event. The industry standard for session leaders is one day of preparation for each day of facilitation. Some complex sessions even have a ratio of two days of preparation for each day of facilitation.

Common time allocations for facilitation assignments:

Workshop Length	Interview Time	Design Time	Total Time
1-day workshop (18 people)	1/2 day	1/2 day	2 days
2-day workshop (18 people)	1 day	1 day	4 days
2-day retreat (60 people)	1 day	3 days	6 days

Time Investment

Establishing Behavioral Norms

Meetings run best when there are clear rules or norms to follow. People may feel reluctant at first to speak up and suggest rules or there may be pressure to start discussing the agenda items.

For these reasons, it's a good strategy to ask group members to suggest norms during the assessment phase. This can be done during one-on-one interviews or via emails. The suggested norms can then be shared and ratified at the end of the feedback meeting.

If you have not created norms during data collection, you can build a set of norms at the meeting to discuss and ratify the agenda. Simply ask members specific norming questions like:

" What rules will ensure that this meeting runs smoothly?"

"What should the rule be about laptops and handhelds?"

"What about side conversations?"

"What should the rule be about bringing up topics not on the agenda?"

Combine responses into a coherent set of meeting guidelines and bring the guidelines forward at the start of the facilitated session.

Negotiating Personal Power

It is also important during the final preparation phase to negotiate for sufficient power to be able to manage the dynamics of the group. This is especially important for internal facilitators.

The most obvious lack of power is experienced by staff who are asked to facilitate a meeting filled with upper-level managers. To gain the power needed to manage the interactions of powerful groups, facilitators always negotiate for the power they will need beforehand.

In addition to helping the group set norms during the feedback session, ask members pointed questions about what's okay for you to say and do during the facilitation. Make sure they understand that you may need to be assertive to keep things on track. Prompt conversation with questions such as:

"If people start to side-chat, run in and out, or talk over each other, what is it okay for me to say and do?

Is it okay for me to tactfully point these things out and steer people back?"

"What if there are arguments or someone goes on for too long? Can I point these things out and suggest what would be better?"

In most cases the group members will tell you that they want you to be assertive and will give you the permission you need to intervene whenever necessary. In some cases they may even go further and ask you to stop them if they fall into ineffective patterns.

Strictly speaking, facilitators do not need the approval of group members to intervene. Managing group interaction is, after all, the job of the facilitator. The reason for negotiating the right to assertively intervene is to set group member expectations. Once members have stated that they want you to assertively manage the meeting dynamics, it gives you the green light you need to step in.

Start by saying something like:

"I'm going to remind you that you asked me to stop you if this happened."

It creates a group norm that protects the facilitator from being seen as overstepping traditional boundaries. Negotiating the right to intervene assertively gives facilitators the green light to do their jobs and protects them from having career-limiting moments.

 Facilitators have no real power, so they have to negotiate the power they need.

Final Preparations

❑ finalize the design and share it with group members

❑ clarify what you and the group are responsible for

❑ negotiate the power needed to manage effectively

❑ check the suitability of the meeting location

❑ help the meeting organizer prepare a letter detailing meeting logistics and the final agenda for distribution

❑ identify all needed materials and supplies

❑ create all workshop materials and handouts

❑ print all materials and handouts

❑ prepare flipchart sheets ahead of time or program the electronic board.

The members of the group are typically responsible for sending notices, arranging and paying for logistics such as accommodations, insuring that a suitable meeting room is available, arranging and paying for printing, keeping clear minutes of the proceedings, transcribing all flip chart notes, monitoring to ensure follow-through on all action plans, and evaluating the results.

4. Starting a Facilitation

You must arrive before the other members of the group. This ensures that there's time to make last-minute seating changes in the room, post the agenda and survey data, test the equipment, and so on. Arriving early also allows you to greet participants as they arrive. Chatting informally with members not only helps break the ice but also gives people an opportunity to get to know you.

Room set-up is critical for facilitated discussions. A large room with modular furniture works best for both large group and subgroup settings. Huge boardroom tables, on the other hand, are detrimental to creating an atmosphere conducive to dialogue. A long table reinforces hierarchical patterns and discourages eye contact. When facilitating large groups, it's best to seat people at round tables spaced evenly around the room. Small table groups of five to eight are ideal.

Start each discussion by specifying: purpose, process and time.

If you are using flip charts, make sure there's ample wall space for posting the notes that will be generated throughout the day. If the design calls for breaking into small-group discussions, you will need an additional easel for each subgroup.

Develop your own approach for beginning a session:

- ❑ introduce yourself and give your brief background
- ❑ clarify the role you'll be playing as the facilitator
- ❑ clarify the roles to be played by other members
- ❑ go around the room and have members introduce themselves by name and perhaps position
- ❑ take care of all housekeeping items
- ❑ conduct a quick warm-up activity to relax the group
- ❑ review any data collected; have key points posted for all to see and answer questions about the data
- ❑ review the agenda; clarify the objectives and desired outcomes of the entire meeting and the meeting's subsections
- ❑ review behavioral norms or meeting guidelines that will be in effect during the session
- ❑ remind group members of the powers they gave you to intervene
- ❑ if the group already has a set of meeting guidelines, review these and add any new norms. You can also ratify the ones that were developed during the design phase. Post the norms in clear view.
- ❑ set up a parking lot sheet on a wall to track digressions
- ❑ make a clear statement about the purpose of the each agenda item; describe each expected outcome
- ❑ describe the process tools and techniques to be used in each discussion
- ❑ set out the timeframe for each agenda item; in some settings, set a timer or appoint a timekeeper
- ❑ start the discussions.

Once the preliminaries have been dealt with, start the first discussion. Remember to begin each new agenda item with a clear Start Sequence.

5. During a Facilitation

The key contribution of the facilitator during any meeting is to provide the necessary structure and guidance so that discussions are consistently effective. Facilitators do not act like passive scribes while members discuss agenda items.

Remember that facilitators are only neutral about the content of discussions. They continually monitor group interaction and intervene whenever they see group productivity decline.

In addition to making interventions, facilitators also periodically make process checks. Refer to page 17 for a more detailed description of the four elements of every process check. These are either made at the halfway point of any discussion or are conducted whenever there are signs that things are not going well.

During all discussions be sure to:

❑ ask positive, energetic, probing questions to further the conversation and engage members

❑ paraphrase continually to acknowledge and clarify

❑ monitor time and maintain an appropriate pace

❑ keep track of ideas by making concise notes

❑ make summaries to restart or end conversations

❑ encourage members to adhere to their ground rules

❑ make interventions if behaviors become ineffective

❑ keep the group on track and park off-topic items

❑ help members objectively discuss opinions

❑ make process checks to test overall effectiveness

❑ stop the action if the discussion spins its wheels, ask members why they're stuck and what will move them

❑ adjust the process and offer additional tools.

6. Ending a Facilitation

A common problem in many meetings is lack of closure. Lots of things are discussed, but there's no clear path forward. One of the facilitator's key contributions is to ensure that decisions are reached and detailed action steps are in place before moving to the next topic or adjourning the meeting.

Some ways to bring effective closure to a meeting:

❑ provide summary statements about what has been decided and record these on a flip chart or electronic board

❑ ensure that each action item is accompanied by detailed action plans

❑ round up items not discussed at the meeting, including those placed in the parking lot, and help members create a plan of action for each

❑ help the group create an agenda for the next meeting

❑ decide on a means of follow-up: written reports or group session

❑ clarify your role in any follow-up meetings

❑ help members decide who will transcribe notes

❑ make digital snapshots of all flip-chart notes as a back-up

❑ post an exit survey to get member views about the session

❑ hand out a written evaluation so that group members can provide more detailed comments about the session and offer you feedback on your work

❑ thank the participants for the opportunity to facilitate.

7. Following Up on a Facilitation

No matter how formal or informal the facilitation process has been, following up with the group is always a good idea. If the facilitation consisted of a brief meeting, you might simply call the group leader to determine the extent to which the session helped the group become more effective. If the session was a major decision-making workshop or retreat, encourage the group leader to send out a written follow-up workshop evaluation to the members.

Unless it was formally agreed that you would conduct the follow-up activity, you can leave any post-session reports to the group's members. This ensures that they, not you, assume accountability for the implementation of the ideas emerging from the session. Your role may be to merely remind the group about the need for follow-up and to provide them with a format for reporting results later. In some cases, you may negotiate with the group to facilitate a follow-up meeting at which post-meeting progress is discussed and evaluated.

Seeking Feedback on Your Facilitation

When an outside facilitator works with a client, it's routine procedure for him or her to seek feedback about his or her personal performance from the person who made the contract. This is done to ensure that the client is satisfied and helps preserve the client relationship.

It's equally important for internal facilitators to seek feedback. They may not be worried about cultivating a client, but they should be thinking about whether or not their work contributed to the overall health of the organization.

Gaining detailed and specific feedback is essential for all facilitators seeking to increase their personal effectiveness. The feedback process can be done in person or over the phone. The format is often as simple as asking fundamental questions like:

"What did I do well?

"What was my most valuable contribution?"

"What did I do during the session that was especially effective?"

"What did I not do well?"

"In what instances could I have done something differently?"

"What specific improvements could I make to my facilitation work to become even more effective?"

FACILITATORS ARE ALWAYS KEENLY AWARE OF THE GROUP DYNAMIC AND WORK HARD TO MAKE SURE THAT ALL VOICES ARE HEARD.

FOUR

WHO CAN FACILITATE

Once the need for facilitation has been identified, there's often confusion about who should take on the role. Should it be an internal staff member, a paid outsider, or the leader of the group?

When to Use an Internal Facilitator

In many organizations, facilitators are considered such an important resource as to warrant the development of a full-time in-house cadre. These are paid organization development consultants who are available to help any team needing assistance.

Some organizations that are unable to maintain full-time facilitators, maintain a group of part-time volunteer facilitators. These are employees who are interested in developing their group process expertise and who voluntarily take on facilitation assignments in other parts of their organization.

Whether they're full-time professionals or part of a volunteer group, internal facilitators enjoy several advantages over external ones, such as:

○ they understand the organization's history and culture

○ they have a stake in the health and success of the organization

○ they're on hand and easy to access

○ they're on salary, so are less costly than hiring out

- they're aware of the resources available within the organization
- they can follow the outcomes of their work and ensure continuity.

Despite the many benefits of using internal facilitators, there are also some drawbacks, such as:

- internal facilitators may lack experience with specific facilitation tools or processes
- even when they're very experienced, they may not be seen as credible inside the organization
- they may have a history with some co-workers, who consequently do not see them as neutral
- they may be stretched too far if there are only a few of them to deal with all of the needs of a large organization
- some discussions may simply be too risky to be tackled by an insider, who then has to stay around and live with the fallout.

 Facilitators don't have to be neutral outsiders.

When to Use an External Facilitator

It's advantageous to use an outside facilitator in a number of situations, most notably when total neutrality is essential and the discussions require the full participation of all members. In addition, external facilitators enjoy several advantages, including:

- they're assumed to be credible
- they may have more experience leading some types of specialized discussions
- people are more likely to trust their neutrality
- they're unencumbered by political or emotional baggage

- they can often afford to take more risks

- they can walk away from the repercussions of sensitive interventions

- they are paid for their efforts, so much can be asked of them.

 External facilitators are automatically given greater credibility.

Using the services of an external facilitator also has drawbacks, including:

- they lack data about the group and the organization, such as its history, and therefore need to do considerable research

- they don't fully understand the personalities involved

- they need to build rapport with the client to establish trust

- they don't get to see the initiatives of the group unfold

- they can be costly to hire, especially for longer projects

- they may be unavailable for follow-up work.

Organizations that have internal facilitators will still bring in externals for selected assignments. This is usually done for assignments that the internal facilitators feel are too sensitive to tackle or that they lack the expertise to conduct. External facilitators are also brought in to allow the internal team to experience a new technique. Either external or internal, all facilitators work according to a well-defined set of steps, outlined in Chapter Three.

When Leaders Facilitate

It was established in Chapter One that the facilitation function was designed to be performed by a neutral third party. This neutrality exists to ensure that the person facilitating is able to focus all of his or her attention on providing structure and to encourage people to speak freely. It's important to note that when an internal facilitator takes on an assignment within the organization, he or she is nonetheless operating as a neutral outsider in relation to the internal client.

Unfortunately, neutral parties simply aren't available every time there's a need for effective process. As a result, the task of designing and managing meetings almost always falls to leaders. This begs the question: *"Can a leader who has an interest in the outcome of a discussion, effectively facilitate the members of his or her own team?"*

The simple answer is yes: Leaders who have a stake in the decisions being made by their teams can nonetheless, provide effective process leadership. The catch is that they have to approach the facilitator role very differently. There are two main reasons for this.

! Leaders can facilitate their own people but must use specific strategies.

First, leaders have a degree of power over the members of their teams. This means that, even when the leader claims to be neutral, team members may be reluctant to speak up and voice opinions that could be contrary to what they think the leader might want to hear.

Second, many leaders have a difficult time switching into the neutral mode. They may want the input of staff, but may be so used to solving problems and making decisions that they can't hold back their opinions.

Given the great need for effective process in every meeting, it's clear that leaders need strategies to provide process to their teams. This means learning to do a delicate balancing act. While it's definitely easier for a neutral party to facilitate, leaders can manage the facilitator role if they're aware of the challenges they face and have strategies to overcome them.

Facilitation Strategies for Leaders

Challenge 1—Leaders often choose the wrong discussions to facilitate. They may mistakenly try to be neutral during a discussion about a topic on which they have most of the expertise. Also, they may try to facilitate an entire meeting, instead of chairing the main portions of the meeting in the usual manner and then selectively facilitating those topics where it's most effective to gain staff input.

Strategy 1—Leaders need to pick the right topics to facilitate.

Challenge 2—Staff may not understand the role of facilitator and could therefore be confused when the leader starts to act in a new way.

Strategy 2—The first few times a leader facilitates, he or she should clearly explain what a facilitator does, the reason for choosing to facilitate at this point in the meeting, and the length of time he or she will be in the role.

The leader needs to be clear that the honest opinions and insights of the members are being sought and that no decision has been made about the matter under discussion. Once group members understand that their leader really is looking for their ideas on a specific topic, they are more likely to accept their leader in the role of a facilitator.

Challenge 3—Group members are going to be justifiably leery of taking part in decision making if they sense that the decision is actually going to be made elsewhere anyway.

Strategy 3—When leaders facilitate, they need to be very clear about the empowerment level of the group members. Leaders need to tell followers who will be making the final decision whether they are making a recommendation that needs final approval or are merely being asked for their ideas as input for a decision that will be made by someone else. When the decision-making context is clarified, people will be more likely to engage.

Meeting Leadership

DIRECTIVE	FACILITATIVE
Be directive and act like a meeting chair:	*Be facilitative for the sections of the meeting:*
▢ to give clear instructions	▢ to gain input of team members
▢ to share your expertise	▢ to create more buy-in and commitment
▢ to tell people about decisions already made	▢ to encourage staff to take the lead
▢ when there's no input on non-negotiable situations	▢ when accountability can be shared
▢ when accountability's not shared	▢ when the ideas of staff are needed and can actually be implemented
▢ when there's no possibility that staff ideas will be implemented	

Also, a leader who feels he or she needs to retain the power to make the final decision on a matter can tell people that he or she is using Level II empowerment. In this mode, the leader gathers input from staff, but clearly signals to them that they are not making the final decision. This allows the leader to be both the facilitator in the meeting and the decider after the meeting. The key is to be totally open that this is what is happening.

A chart that's useful for clarifying decision authority is the **Empowerment Chart** on the next page. Leaders should share this chart with their teams and then clarify the specific level that applies to each agenda item before they start.

Challenge 4—The leader sets out to facilitate, but the moment group members propose an idea that seems flawed, he or she falls out of the role and takes control.

Strategy 4—Leaders need to accept that facilitating can result in the group coming up with ideas that have flaws. Rather than stepping in to overturn their suggestions, leaders must help group members apply critical thinking skills so that they can discover the gaps themselves.

Empowerment Levels

Level I	**Telling:** Staff are told about an outcome and have no input
Level II	**Consulting:** Staff are consulted for their input, but the final decision will be made elsewhere.
Level III	**Participating:** Staff are asked for their ideas and can create action plans, but these plans need approval before they can be implemented.
Level IV	**Delegating:** Staff can make decisions and act on their ideas without any further approvals.

* For more information on using the Empowerment Chart refer to Chapter Seven.

The leader can help members identify the traits of an effective solution, then have group members use those criteria to test their proposal. Another approach when members seem to be making a low-quality decision is to help members objectively list both the upside and downside of their ideas. The leader can then facilitate discussions to help members find solutions to overcome the weaknesses they identified in their own proposal.

Challenge 5—When a leader asks a question, his or her staff will naturally try to figure out whether there's a motive behind the question or guess what the leader might have in mind.

Strategy 5—Leaders must ask questions in such a neutral manner that no one can possibly guess at a motive behind them. For example, a leader can ask two questions at once: one that goes in one direction and one that goes in another. This can sound like: *"Tell me why this is a good idea; then I want you to tell me why this might be the worst thing to do."*

Challenge 6—People may stay quiet with the leader in the room to avoid saying things that they think the leader won't like.

Strategy 6—Leaders have to be on the lookout for opportunities to choose techniques that don't require open discussion. These techniques allow for ideas to be shared both silently and anonymously.

- Brainstorm on sticky notes, then use multi-voting to prioritize suggestions and arrive at the best action.

- Post issues on walls and then allow people to wander from topic to topic, sharing views with members of the small groups gathered at the same topic.

- A neutral approach to making decisions is to have group members anonymously provide their rating of an idea on a decision grid.

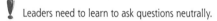 Leaders need to learn to ask questions neutrally.

For many of these processes, the leader can set up the exercise and then participate as a group member, since no discussion actually takes place.

Challenge 7—The group needs structure to effectively discuss a complex topic, but the leader needs to be in the discussion and no one else is available to facilitate.

Strategy 7—When the input of the leader is essential to the discussion, he or she may only be able to step into the neutral facilitator role for the start of the discussion to help the group clarify the purpose, the process, and the time.

When a leader can't facilitate he or she should at least establish the Start Sequence and offer process tools.

Once the Start Sequence is in place, the leader can announce that he or she is stepping out of the facilitator role to take part in the discussion. While this is far from

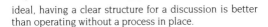

ideal, having a clear structure for a discussion is better than operating without a process in place.

Challenge 8—The group needs structure, but the group is too small to lose someone to play the neutral role.

Strategy 8—In situations when no one is available to facilitate, the group can use a strategy known as shared facilitation. This involves taking the roles that a facilitator would normally perform and dividing them among the members so that everyone has at least one role to play.

After the leader has established the Start Sequence, he or she divides up the tasks that the facilitator would normally perform, such as keeping track of time, recording ideas, pointing out digressions and parking them, calling on quiet people, summarizing points, identifying when the group is stuck, and so forth.

Challenge 9—Leaders' expertise is always in demand, so they are seldom free to step into the facilitator role.

Strategy 9—Whenever leaders facilitate, they should try to help their people learn to facilitate so that facilitation duties can be rotated. The best way to do this is for leaders to model facilitation and then debrief the various functions so that members can understand the techniques involved. By modeling facilitation techniques, leaders can teach others how to facilitate so that they can share the role and won't always have to stand outside the group.

Once all team members have mastered the basics, the facilitator role can be rotated so that everyone learns to use process tools and becomes skilled at managing complex group interactions. This will do a great deal to build the leadership capacity of all members.

Facilitation Strategies for Leaders

BEST	WORST
□ Select the specific discussions that need to be facilitated.	□ Facilitate when you feel like it.
□ Tell people you are facilitating and explain the role clearly.	□ Let people guess at whether you're facilitating or not.
□ Clearly state the empowerment level of staff in each discussion.	□ Neglect to clarify whether members are deciding or just being consulted.
□ Be consistent once in the role; don't leap back and forth.	□ Periodically make strong points while facilitating.
□ Avoid leading questions.	□ Ask the questions that lead people to the ideas you like.
□ Use tools that create objectivity and anonymity.	□ Make people stand up and take a stand publicly.
□ Use neutral body language.	□ Let how you feel about their ideas show through.
□ Always set up a Start Sequence, even when not facilitating.	□ Have discussions without clear parameters.
□ Manage group effectiveness, even when not facilitating.	□ Fail to notice how people are interacting.
□ Share facilitation tasks with group members.	□ Be the only skilled facilitator on your team.
□ Teach others to facilitate.	□ Do not teach anyone else.

Facilitation as a Leadership Style

Centuries of directive leadership have created a culture in many organizations where those at the front line are viewed only as doers and totally underutilized as thinkers. This directive leadership style may still work in some settings, but is largely ineffective in today's knowledge-driven organizations.

Workplaces need to harness the intelligence, commitment, and energy of all their members. This level of engagement can only be fostered by a shift in leadership—from telling to asking and from controlling to facilitating.

 Leaders can shift their styles by facilitating more and directing less.

When leaders shift their approach from controlling and directing to facilitating and empowering, they may feel as though they're giving up control. In reality, there's a substantial amount of power and control built into the role of facilitator. The difference is that this power is exerted indirectly, through the application of process, rather than through control over content.

Consider the following examples of how process can be used to manage in specific situations:

Leader Options

SITUATIONS	DIRECTIVE Approach	FACILITATIVE Approach
▫ Members argue.	▫ Give them a pep talk about getting along.	▫ Have members create rules to manage disagreements.
▫ A poor decision is made.	▫ Overturn it, then explain later.	▫ Have members critique their decision using objective criteria.
▫ Members overstep their authority.	▫ Rein them in, then supervise more carefully.	▫ Expand empowerment to meet the needs of specific situations.

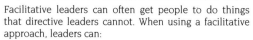

Facilitative leaders can often get people to do things that directive leaders cannot. When using a facilitative approach, leaders can:

- help groups to identify and commit to achieving ambitious goals
- build and maintain high-performance teams
- engage groups in creative thinking
- settle conflicts between groups
- help staff to resolve complex problems
- manage interpersonal dynamics.

A neutral role is actually very freeing. When leaders stop giving all the answers, staff must be resourceful and learn to bring answers. Instead of complying with orders, they participate in creating strategies and plans. When given decision-making authority, they weigh options more carefully. When a leader adopts a more facilitative approach, group members are challenged to take on more. This develops their autonomy and brings out their leadership potential.

One of the most important outcomes of leaders taking a facilitative approach is that it encourages dialogue. When leaders ask questions, they foster conversation. This gives staff an opportunity to vent, to challenge, and to explore new ideas. The net result is a greater sense of partnership.

Additional Role Challenges

Both internal and external facilitators encounter situations in which they feel that they lack the authority to effectively manage the group's process. For the external facilitator this can be when the client second-guesses the design and meddles throughout the assignment. For internal facilitators this lack of authority often stems from the fact that they're facilitating staff whose rank is higher than their own. Here are some common role dilemmas and solutions.

Facilitating Difficult Clients

They hire you for your expertise, but then they meddle in your design. They may do this in advance, or they may try to change the design midstream. You make interventions, but they don't listen. They just expect you to adjust to whatever they throw at you.

What's going on? They want you to do what they want you to do. They are not very good at following while others lead. They feel that because they hired you, you must do as they dictate.

What to do about it: During the assessment phase interviews, ask each group member for suggestions about the rules of conduct that should be in place during the facilitation. Ask individuals to tell you about the things that happen in the group that can make it less effective. Ask for specific suggestions or norms that could be put into place to eliminate these behaviors.

At the start of the facilitation share the rules that were suggested by the group members during the interviews. Ratify these rules and post them in clear sight so that you can use them to intervene if people violate them.

When presenting to the group, clarify that you will be leaving the content totally to them, but that you must be in control of the process. Explain that you may consult them, but that the decision to use a specific tool or approach needs to rest with you. Gain a firm commitment to this and post it along with the group norms. If people start to meddle, thank them for their input, then politely remind them that the design is your area of expertise.

This avoids clashes between the role of the content leader and role of the process leader during the session.

Facilitating Senior Managers

You're asked to facilitate for a group of senior managers. This group needs your help, but then resists your efforts to provide structure. They second-guess your approach, are distracted by laptops, go off on tangents, argue, and run in and out of the meeting. Because they're all senior to you, you don't feel that you can intervene or assert the process.

What's going on? The hierarchy of the organization is spilling over into the facilitation arena. The managers are not used to being facilitated and do not have a clear understanding about the role of a neutral third party.

What to do about it: Clearly explain the role of the facilitator to the group members during the design phase. Help group members understand that you're only neutral about the content and that it is within the boundaries of your role to be assertive about the process.

 Facilitators need to negotiate specific powers when dealing with senior management groups.

Also engage the members in setting very specific norms to govern behavior at the session. Ratify these rules at the start of the meeting and then immediately negotiate some power for yourself. Ask questions like:

"What is it okay for me to say or do if I notice that the group's not following its own rules? Can I stop the action and point it out? Can I suggest what would be better?"

"What if I sense that a technique or approach is not working? Can I change it?"

"Can we agree that you're in charge of the content of the discussion, but that I'm managing how the meeting is run?"

When group members agree to these things, they are essentially giving you the power you need to manage the group dynamic. This green light from them protects you. Facilitators don't actually need approval to intervene or manage the process. They already have that authority in the job description. Asking the group for specific powers to intervene and manage the process is simply done to make it less risky to facilitate senior people assertively.

Facilitating Colleagues

You sit through meeting after terrible meeting. You wish that you or someone could just start to facilitate, but do you have the authority to step in?

What's going on? There's a total lack of process and the leader has no idea how to provide structure. No one at the meeting has any idea that the group needs facilitation.

What to do about it: You can work at three levels to provide structure. The first level is the most covert. Simply provide facilitation support from your seat as it's needed. Periodically mention the time, ask quiet people for their ideas, ask probing questions, point out digressions, help people understand differing views, and so forth.

At the second level, you can speak up and offer the group help when it's struggling. Offer a tool or technique. Wait until members agree that they want your help. Then step in to structure the discussion. At the end of that activity, rejoin the group. The general rule is that if you offer facilitation and members accept, you have been given the role.

At the third level, approach the leader and ask him or her to allow you to facilitate all or specific portions of an upcoming meeting. If the leader is reluctant, tell him or her that learning to facilitate is one of your personal learning objectives and that practice is essential.

Manage the session according to the steps outlined in Chapter Three. At the end of the facilitation activities, help the group evaluate the outcome of your work. Hopefully, this will raise members' awareness about the need for a more structured approach to their meetings.

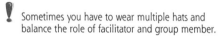

Facilitating Tiny Groups

There are lots of meetings attended by only three or four people. If four people are making a decision and one of them assumes the facilitator's role, this removes a valuable resource from the conversation.

What's going on? There is no neutral outsider available and the group is too small to be able to afford to lose a person to the process role.

> Sometimes you have to wear multiple hats and balance the role of facilitator and group member.

What to do about it: There are a number of solutions to this dilemma:

- set out the process, establish the Start Sequence, and then rejoin the group. Then divide the facilitator role among members with one person watching the time, another noticing digressions, someone recording ideas, and so forth, using the shared facilitation tool mentioned earlier.

- stay in the facilitator role, but write down ideas and give them to a colleague to represent

- stay in the facilitator role and balance the role of facilitator and group member by adding comments only after others have offered their ideas

- facilitate, but take off the facilitator hat periodically to step out of the role to add comments.

Since all group interactions are more effective when attention has been paid to the process, it's very important that facilitation should not be withheld just because the conditions are less than ideal. There will never be a time when there's a neutral third party available to run every meeting, so leaders and team members who understand facilitation will need to find ways to add process elements to their meetings.

Chapter **FIVE**

Knowing Your Participants

Getting to know the people you'll be working with is an essential first step in designing any effective meeting. Before you facilitate, you need to know whether the people coming to the meeting are:

- ❏ total strangers who have never met before and won't be together again after this single, special-purpose meeting

- ❏ total strangers or people who only have a passing acquaintance with each other, but who will be working together again after this meeting

- ❏ a group of people who know each other, have interacted for some time, and get along well

- ❏ a group in turmoil that meets periodically and either spins its wheels in frustration or becomes embroiled in conflicts that are rarely resolved

- ❏ a high-performance team with a solid track record of achievements, made up of members with highly developed people skills who are good at managing their internal group dynamics.

Conducting an Assessment

Experienced facilitators never take a group or situation for granted! They know that surface appearances may not be accurate. They also know that what they are initially told may not be totally accurate.

It's very important, therefore, to do careful background research and design a process that matches the group's actual circumstances. This research is done using one or more of the following techniques:

○ One-on-one interviews—These allow you to question people about the state of the group and member interactions. This is the best way to get people to be open and candid when there are sensitive issues.

○ Group interviews or focus groups—This is an effective strategy when the subject is not sensitive and when there are too many people to interview singly. Group interviews let you observe the group dynamics before the actual facilitated session.

○ Surveys—These allow anonymous gathering of information from all group members. They make it possible to compile answers to the same questions from each member. They also generate quantifiable data.

○ Group observation—This involves attending a group meeting to watch people interact. This is the best way to learn about the interpersonal dynamics of members. Group observation is most helpful when conducting team intervention in mature groups.

Always take the proper time to get to know participants to understand their needs and organizational content.

Assessment Questions

Whether you are asking questions in one-on-one interviews or in survey format, the following questions will be helpful in preparing for a facilitated session:

○ What's the history of the group?
○ What's the proudest achievement of the members?
○ How familiar are members with each other?
○ Are there clear goals?

- Are there team rules or norms?
- In meetings, does everyone participate or do a few dominate?
- To what extent is there a high level of openness and honesty among members?
- Do members listen to and support each other's ideas?
- How does the group handle differing views or conflict?
- How are important decisions made?
- Do people usually leave meetings feeling like something has been achieved?
- How would you describe the group atmosphere?
- Are meetings thoroughly planned and structured or are they basically freewheeling?
- Does the group ever stop to evaluate how it's doing and make corrections?
- What are the best and worst things about the group?
- How do people feel about being part of this group?
- Describe a recent incident that illustrates how members typically interact.
- Are there any reasons why members might not be open or say what they really think?
- Why do you need facilitation support? Is there any opposition to this?
- What's the worst thing that could happen at this meeting? What could be done to ensure that this doesn't happen?
- What advice would you give me in planning this session? Is there a particular pitfall that I need to be aware of?

On the following page, you will find a survey that can be used to assess the internal climate of any group.

Group Assessment Survey

1. How familiar are members of this group with each other?

1	2	3	4	5
Passing acquaintances		Some of us familiar		High-performance team

2. Are there clear goals for the group?

1	2	3	4	5
No stated goals		Unsure about the goals		We have clear goals

3. Is there a clear set of rules to manage interactions?

1	2	3	4	5
No norms exist	We have but don't use our norms			We have & use our norms

4. Describe the typical participation pattern.

1	2	3	4	5
Few people dominate	Participation varies topic to topic			Every voice is heard

5. How much honesty and openness is there in this group?

1	2	3	4	5
People hide what they really think		We are somewhat open		We are very open and honest

6. How good are members at listening, supporting, and encouraging each other?

1	2	3	4	5
We don't do this at all		We try but don't always succeed		We are consistently supportive

7. How do members often handle differences of opinion?

1	2	3	4	5
Lots of emotional arguing		It varies	We always debate objectively & respectfully	

8. How are important decisions usually made?

1	2	3	4	5
Lots of voting & giving in		Our approach varies	We strive for consensus	

9. Does the group usually end its meetings with a sense of achievement and clear action plans?

1	2	3	4	5
	Never		Sometimes		Always

10. How would you describe the atmosphere among members?

1	2	3	4	5
Hostile and tense		Satisfactory	Totally relaxed & harmonious	

11. How would you describe the group's meetings?

1	2	3	4	5
Unstructured & waste of time		Satisfactory	Well planned & productive	

12. Does the group ever stop and evaluate how it's doing and then take action to improve?

1	2	3	4	5
	Never		Sporadically		Consistently

Note: *Refer to the instructions about how to do survey feedback in Chapter Ten.*

Comparing Groups to Teams

There are significant differences between groups and teams. A group is a collection of people who come together to communicate, tackle a problem, or coordinate an event. Groups tend to be run by a chairperson, according to pre-published rules of order. A team runs itself by guidelines created by the members. Some characteristics of groups are:

o individual members operate under their own separate parameters and work to achieve individual goals

o groups usually operate by externally set procedures such as the traditional rules of order

o group members usually have separate roles and responsibilities and tend to work on their own

o individuals in groups operate at various levels of empowerment depending on their position in the organization.

Since group members typically pursue their own individual goals, groups tend to exhibit "I"-centered behavior when debating. This generally makes a group more competitive and argumentative than a true team.

 It's important to know whether you're facilitating a team or a group.

How Is a Team Different from a Group?

In contrast to a group, a team is a collection of people who achieve a clear and compelling common goal that they defined. To the members of a true team, that goal is more important than their own individual pursuits. It's this that gives teams cohesion. A team also creates a set of norms or rules of conduct that define the team's culture.

Team members also jointly plan work and coordinate roles much more than groups do. Their work lives are linked together, and they depend on each other. When team members have differences of opinion, they tend to debate the ideas rather than argue points of view. They aren't out to gain personal victory, but to arrive at the best solution for the good of the whole.

Groups generally have only the level of authority inherent in their position within the organization. Teams seek and attain higher levels of empowerment. Because members draw on each other to make better decisions, a team typically evolves toward greater autonomy in managing its work.

Group/Team Comparison Chart

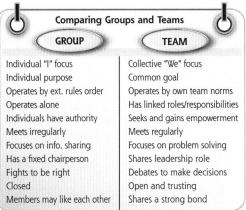

Comparing Groups and Teams

GROUP	TEAM
Individual "I" focus	Collective "We" focus
Individual purpose	Common goal
Operates by ext. rules order	Operates by own team norms
Operates alone	Has linked roles/responsibilities
Individuals have authority	Seeks and gains empowerment
Meets irregularly	Meets regularly
Focuses on info. sharing	Focuses on problem solving
Has a fixed chairperson	Shares leadership role
Fights to be right	Debates to make decisions
Closed	Open and trusting
Members may like each other	Shares a strong bond

Do All Groups Need to Become Teams?

The simple answer is no. While teams have some distinct advantages over groups, not all groups should be developed into teams. It is advantageous to do team building with any group if:

- there's a need to create a high level of cohesion and commitment to a common goal

- there's an ongoing task for the group to accomplish

- a consistent set of people will be working closely over an extended period

- members need to link and coordinate their roles closely

- higher empowerment levels would improve effectiveness and performance.

As a facilitator, you should be aware that you will probably work with more unstructured groups than with real teams who have been through a team-building process.

 Not all groups need to become teams, but all groups can be encouraged to act like teams.

*Getting a Group to **Act** like a Team*

Incorporate the following key team-building activities into the agenda:

- getting people to participate in creating a clear goal for the session or topic being discussed

- creating a set of norms or rules to guide conduct, posting these rules and encouraging members to use them to maintain effective behaviors

- clarifying roles and responsibilities for all action plans generated by the group

- clarifying all accountabilities to ensure that everyone is clear about expected results

- training members in effective behaviors such as how to handle conflict and make decisions

- conducting process checks, building in feedback loops, and other evaluation mechanisms

Chapter SIX

CREATING PARTICIPATION

Imagine yourself at the start of a meeting with a group of people you barely know, in which nothing is working. No one is answering questions. Some people look bored. Others seem openly uncomfortable. Everyone looks nervously at the leader whenever you ask a question. You start to wonder how you're going to get through the rest of the session!

Given the pressures of today's workplace, it would be naïve to go into most meetings assuming that people will automatically be enthusiastic and engaged.

 Anticipate the potential blocks to active participation and come armed with strategies to overcome them.

Consider these main barriers to participation:

❑ people may tire from attending too many meetings

❑ some participants may be exhausted from overwork

❑ some members may be confused about the topic

❑ there may be a lack of commitment to the topic

❑ some people may be insecure about speaking up

❑ talkative members may shut down quieter people

❑ junior staff may be reluctant to speak up in front of those they consider to be their superiors

❑ there may be a low level of trust and openness in the group

- ❑ some traumatic event may have occurred recently that has left people feeling stressed or withdrawn
- ❑ the organization may have a history of not listening to or supporting employee suggestions.

Before the meeting or workshop, find out:

- ❑ whether the participants are used to group discussion
- ❑ how committed people are to the topic
- ❑ how they feel about speaking in front leaders/peers
- ❑ whether relationships among participants are healthy or strained
- ❑ if there has been a recent layoff, personal tragedy, or other event that might distract participants
- ❑ if members have well-developed group skills such as listening, debating, decision making, etc.
- ❑ whether the organization is likely to support the group's ideas.

Creating the Conditions for Full Participation

As basic prerequisites for full participation group members should:

- ❑ feel relaxed with the other participants
- ❑ understand the topic under discussion
- ❑ have had some say in the planning process
- ❑ feel committed to the topic
- ❑ have the information and knowledge needed for fruitful discussion
- ❑ feel safe in expressing their opinions
- ❑ be free from interference or undue influence
- ❑ trust and have confidence in the facilitator
- ❑ be comfortable and at ease in the meeting room
- ❑ feel that the organization will support their ideas.

A good rule is that the more resistant a group is likely to be, the more necessary it is to hold interviews or focus groups with members beforehand to let them voice their concerns so that you can become aware of blocks.

 Be clear about your role, especially with groups unaccustomed to working with facilitators.

Removing the Blocks to Participation

Ensuring that people participate actively is a primary facilitator responsibility. There's no excuse for running a meeting that a few people dominate or in which half the group sits in silent withdrawal. **Here are some strategies to encourage involvement.**

Break the Ice

Even in a group in which members know one another, they need to engage in icebreakers to set a warm and supportive tone. With groups of strangers, icebreakers help people get to know each other and help to remove barriers to speaking in front of strangers.

Clarify Your Role

In situations when people seldom work with outside facilitators, they may hold back if they're confused about your role. Near the beginning of any facilitation, tell participants why you're there and what you'll be doing. Be clear about your neutrality and explain that your role is to make sure everyone is committed to the work of the group and that discussions stay on track. This will help people feel that you are there to support them.

Share your hopes for a successful meeting, so people know you intend to help make it a productive session. Don't be afraid to brag about yourself a bit. Some participants will be more likely to speak up if they have confidence in your skills.

Clarify the Topic

At the start, ensure that each topic is clearly defined. If the meeting is being called to solve a problem, ensure that there's a clear problem statement. Regardless of the type of session, a clear statement that describes the purpose of the meeting is a must. Refer back to Chapter One for a clear Start Sequence.

You add to topic clarity by having a well-defined outcome statement for each discussion. This means helping the group to agree on what they hope to achieve. This aligns the participants.

You can ensure topic clarity by:

❑ reviewing the history of the situation so that everyone understands the need for the meeting

❑ sharing any input members gave during surveys, focus groups, or interviews to emphasize member participation in creating the agenda

❑ engaging participants in ratifying a purpose statement to ensure understanding and commitment

❑ stating the goal of the facilitation so everyone is clear about the desired outcome.

Always be alert to the fact that even a crystal-clear purpose can quickly become cloudy. Members can become sidetracked or bring in new elements that obscure the purpose of the meeting. Check often to make sure that members remain clear about the goal and haven't become confused.

 Even a clear purpose can become obscure.

It's quite common for facilitators to have to redesign a session in midstream. That's what makes facilitating such a challenge! The wise facilitator is always open to making changes. Forcing a group to continue a discussion that no longer makes sense, just because it's on the agenda, is a sure formula for disaster.

Create Buy-In

In today's work environment, it's folly to run any meeting without gaining buy-in from the participants.

In many organizations, speculation about layoffs is rampant. People may also be weary after wave upon wave of new initiatives. These and other forms of turbulence have left people cynical. They may be feeling vulnerable. They are often working longer hours than in the past. In many organizations, employee morale is low, while distrust levels are high.

Facilitators who naïvely think that people are automatically going to be keen and enthusiastic about coming to their session are in for a shock. Determine how many of these harsh realities could be a factor:

❑ people are working extra hours and don't know how they'll find the time to attend the session

❑ facilitated meetings usually generate many action plans; this is extra work no one wants

❑ the organization may not support the ideas generated by employees; priorities could shift tomorrow

❑ employees may feel that the improvements gained will only benefit the organization.

On the simplest level, getting people to commit is achieved by asking them to answer the universal buy-in question: "What's in it for me?" The most basic buy-in exercise is to pair participants at the start of a session and ask them to spend several minutes discussing two questions in relation to the purpose of the meeting:

"What's the gain for the organization?"

"How will you personally benefit?"

After the partner discussion, participants can recount their own or their partner's responses. Record all comments on a flip chart or electronic board.

The responses to the second question amount to the participants' psychological buy-in to the session. This process seems simple, and is actually very effective.

You will need to vary the buy-in question for different situations. To create buy-in for a process-improvement exercise, ask members:

"How will your work life be easier if we simplify this process?"

To create buy-in for joining a team, ask members:

"What are the benefits for you personally if you become a member of this team?"

To create buy-in for learning a new skill, ask members:

"How is learning to operate the new software going to benefit you?"

If the pre-workshop diagnostics reveal that participants feel that there are lots of reasons for them not to participate, you'll need to spend more time on the buy-in activity.

 Some leaders need to be coached ahead of time so they do not dominate.

In these cases of heightened levels of resistance, you can add two questions to the partner buy-in exercise:

"What's blocking me personally from participating? Why might I be reluctant?"

"What will it take to overcome these blocks? Under what conditions, and with what support, will I consider giving this my total commitment?"

When you record member responses to the two questions above, you'll actually be negotiating group member participation. People may say they'll participate if they receive assurances of senior management support or that they'll participate wholeheartedly if they receive training or other needed assistance. Having their conditions on the table lets you assess the extent to which participants are feeling blocked.

The problem with identifying the blocks is, of course, that you may not be in a position to negotiate some of these items. If you anticipate strong resistance, it's best to uncover the blocks in the planning phase. This allows the time that may be needed to negotiate support issues before the session. The results of these negotiations can then be presented at the beginning of the session to help relieve concerns and help people move forward with commitment. In high-resistance situations, managers and even senior managers may have to be present at the start of a meeting to respond to the needs expressed by the members.

Identify Organizational Support

If the pre-workshop interviews reveal that people are worried that the session might be an exercise in futility, be sure to express these concerns to the appropriate manager. There's nothing worse than having members balk at the start of a workshop because they feel that their ideas won't be supported. If organizational barriers can be dealt with before the session, that will help create a much more positive environment.

Another common strategy is to have a senior manager attend the kick-off portion of the meeting to offer his or her personal assurance of support for the group's efforts. If this isn't possible, a memo or letter from the senior manager expressing strong support is a help.

If there's no senior management support and barriers are a major concern, it's important to surface these issues and discuss them, rather than pretend they don't exist. Set aside time at the end of the workshop to identify the barriers, analyze them, and generate solutions for getting around them. This way, members will feel that the discussions have been honest and that they have strategies for dealing with the realities they face.

Managing the Participation of Leaders

If you're acting as an external facilitator, you'll often be asked to plan and manage meetings in which the group's leader is present. This leader may be the person who contacted you and you may consider this person your client.

Leaders are accustomed to influencing the outcome of meetings. For this reason it isn't unheard of for a leader to ask a facilitator to lead a discussion in the direction of a predetermined outcome that he or she favors. The harsh reality is that some people see facilitation as a sophisticated tool for manipulating others.

To avoid misunderstandings, the facilitator and leader need to meet ahead of time to discuss a number of key points. The leader needs to be tactfully told that:

- while the leader is very important, a facilitator's client is always the whole group, including the leader
- facilitation is a democratic undertaking where the leader agrees to accept decisions made by the whole group
- facilitators needs to be able to contact participants before the session via interviews/surveys to gain input.

If the pre-session interviews with staff reveal that the leader is domineering or that staff are reluctant to speak in the leader's presence, it's a wise strategy to speak with the leader before the session and ask him or her to hold back. Every experienced facilitator can recount stories of situations in which the group leader had to be taken aside at a break and asked to temper his or her participation.

One strategy is to have the leader attend a kick-off session, pledge support, and then leave while the staff works. At the end, the leader returns to hear final recommendations, give any needed approvals, and offer to act as an ongoing sponsor of member activities.

If you're lucky enough to have a group whose leader is open and regarded as a valuable colleague by team members, encourage him or her to play an active role in the entire discussion. After all, one of the reasons leaders bring in facilitators is so they can participate and offer their expertise to the group.

Help Participants Prepare

People often hold back at meetings because they aren't prepared. Make sure that the purpose of each meeting is clearly communicated ahead of time so that people have time to prepare. If a meeting is complex, identify who needs to do which portion of the homework. When people do adequate pre-work, they gain confidence and participate more actively.

Create Targeted Norms

All groups need guidelines to ensure a cooperative and supportive climate. All groups should have a set of core norms that were created with the input of all the members. Having a basic set of norms may not, however, be sufficient to handle the task of getting through a sensitive conversation. If this happens the group will need to create specific, targeted norms to ensure that members feel safe enough to participate freely. Safety norms are an example of targeted norms. In this case, norms are created to reduce the risk to participants for speaking out. Help members create safety norms by asking:

> *"What rules are needed for today's conversation to ensure that everyone can confidently share what's on their mind?"*

> *"Under what conditions are you able to speak freely?"*

Some examples of safety norms are:

○ everything will be said with positive intention to improve the team and the workplace

○ all ideas will be listened to with respect

○ all discussions will be held strictly confidential: What's said here stays here

- both people and issues will be handled with sincerity

- there will be no retaliation on the basis of anything that is said during this meeting

- no one will personally attack another person

- all feedback must be phrased in a constructive manner and be aimed at helping the other person or the team

- if anyone feels emotionally stressed, he or she can call time out or request a change in how a topic is being handled

- everyone will use neutral body language and avoid things like finger-pointing, eye rolling, or sighing

- instead of arguing personal points, we will listen to and acknowledge each other's ideas first

- anyone can call a time out if he or she is confused about the topic or feels that the discussion is going off track.

We all know that these rules will be most effective if they're suggested by the group members themselves. There's one exception to this general rule, however.

If you are about to conduct an intervention with a group of people who are not only extremely dysfunctional but also unlikely to suggest effective rules for themselves, you will have to suggest the rules. In these types of circumstances, clearly state that you will be unable to facilitate unless these rules are accepted by each member. Read the rules aloud at the start of the session and then go around the entire group and ask each person if he or she is willing to adhere to the rules. This will not only set the right climate, but will provide also you with the leverage you need to intervene if people act inappropriately.

Targeted norms may also be necessary in a variety of other situations.

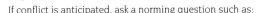

If conflict is anticipated, ask a norming question such as:

> *"What rules are needed today to ensure that we have healthy debates instead of heated arguments"*?

If any members of a group are reluctant to participate, ask:

> *"What would encourage participation and make everyone feel that their ideas are important?"*

If the group has trouble staying on track, ask:

> *"How do we ensure that this meeting stays on track and on time?"*

Make Eye Contact

This is a simple but very important technique to improve participation. Make eye contact with everyone, not just the active participants. By looking directly at quiet people, you're telling them that they haven't been forgotten. The eye contact must, of course, be friendly and encouraging, not piercing and intimidating.

Use Humor

Everybody enjoys a good laugh, and humor is a great way to create an open atmosphere. You can introduce humor into your sessions by having people reveal amusing anecdotes about themselves, showing cartoons, or stopping periodically for a team game. Running jokes and amusing comments are all useful as long as they're in proper proportion and don't detract from the focus of the session.

Set Up the Room to Encourage Participation

Theater-style seating is the worst possible arrangement for facilitating an interactive discussion. People automatically assume that they'll be spoken at. It also discourages people from looking at each other.

Large boardroom tables have an especially stifling effect on people. This is very unfortunate, as many large companies have huge boardroom tables stuck squarely in the middle of many of their best meeting rooms. If a boardroom-style space is your only option for your session, break people into pairs, trios, and foursomes as often as possible to keep everyone talking.

Small tables arranged in a large horseshoe for whole-group sessions is a good arrangement for groups with more than twelve members.

 Room set-up is important for encouraging participation.

When a group has more than twelve people, it's important to break it into smaller groups of five to six people. People can sit in their small groups, even when the whole group is in session. Small groups always help break the ice and create a more private forum for discussions.

Clarify Your Role

People sometimes hold back if they're confused about your role. Near the beginning of any facilitation, tell participants why you're there and what you'll be doing. Be clear that you'll make sure everyone is heard, that you'll work hard to keep discussions on track, and that you'll be remaining neutral on all topics.

High-Participation Techniques

There are many excellent techniques available to get even the most reluctant and shy participant to play an active part. These techniques offer anonymity to members and generate lots of energy.

 Creating activity and buzz in the room brings people together.

Discussion Partners

This simple technique can be used as a way of starting any discussion. After posing a question to a large group, ask everyone to find a partner to discuss the question for a few minutes. Have people report on what they talked about.

Tossed Salad

Place an inexpensive plastic salad bowl, or an empty cardboard box, or as a last resort put the little waste basket on the table. Give out small slips of paper and ask people to write down one good idea per slip. Have them toss the slips into the bowl and "toss the salad." Then pass around the bowl so that each person can take out as many slips as he or she tossed in. Go around the table and have people share ideas before discussing and refining the most promising ideas as a group.

Issues and Answers

When faced with a long list of issues to tackle, rather than attempting to problem solve all of them as a whole group, which may take too long, post the problems around the room. Put only one issue on each sheet of flip-chart paper or section of the electronic board.

Ask all members to go to one of the issue sheets and discuss that problem with whomever else was drawn to that topic. Make sure people are distributed evenly, with at least three people per issue. You can use chairs, but this works best as a stand-up activity.

Allow up to five minutes for the subgroups to analyze the situation. Have them make notes on the top half of each flip-chart sheet. Periodically ask everyone to move to another flip chart sheet. When they switch, ask them to read the analysis made by the first group and to add any additional ideas. Keep this under five minutes. Keep people circulating until everyone has added ideas to all sheets.

Once the analysis round is complete, ask everyone to return to the original issue he or she started with. Ask them to generate and record solutions to their respective issues on the bottom half of the sheet. Once again circulate people until everyone has added ideas on all of the sheets. To end the process have everyone check off the one to three solutions they think are best.

Talk Circuit

This technique works best in a large crowd because it creates a strong buzz and lets people get to know each other. Start by posing a question to the group and then allow quiet time for each person to write his or her own response.

Ask everyone to sit knee-to-knee with a partner and share ideas. Have one person speak while the other acts as the facilitator. After two to three minutes, stop the interaction and have partners reverse their roles. After two to three more minutes, stop the discussions.

Ask everyone to find a new partner and repeat the process, but in slightly less time. Stop the action and then have everyone repeat the process with a third partner.

In the final round allow only one minute per person. When the partner discussions are over, share the ideas as a whole group and record them.

Pass the Envelope

Give each person an envelope filled with blank slips of paper. Pose a question or challenge to the group, and then have everyone write down as many ideas as they can within the given time frame and put the slips into the envelope. Tell people to pass the envelopes, either to the next person or in all directions, and when the passing stops, ask them to read the contents of the envelopes they received.

Place participants in pairs and have them discuss the ideas in their envelope. What ideas did they receive? What are the positives and negatives of each idea? What other ideas should they add? Combine pairs to form groups of four and ask them to further refine the contents of their respective envelopes into practical action plans. Hold a plenary to collect ideas.

Group Participation Survey

Rate how your group currently manages the participation. Be totally honest and anonymous. The results will be tabulated and fed back to the group for their assessment.

1. At our meetings people feel free to express any idea regardless of who's present.

1	2	3	4	5
totally disagree	disagree somewhat	not sure	agree somewhat	totally agree

2. Everyone feels totally relaxed.

1	2	3	4	5
totally disagree	disagree somewhat	not sure	agree somewhat	totally agree

3. The members of our group are always clear about the purpose of discussions.

1	2	3	4	5
totally disagree	disagree somewhat	not sure	agree somewhat	totally agree

4. People do the homework and come to meetings prepared.

1	2	3	4	5
totally disagree	disagree somewhat	not sure	agree somewhat	totally agree

5. Members listen to and respect each other's views.

1	2	3	4	5
totally disagree	disagree somewhat	not sure	agree somewhat	totally agree

6. Members appreciate each other's different strengths. Everyone is valued for his or her specific skills.

1	2	3	4	5
totally disagree	disagree somewhat	not sure	agree somewhat	totally agree

7. Members recognize and accept individual differences.

1	2	3	4	5
totally disagree	disagree somewhat	not sure	agree somewhat	totally agree

8. The organization fully supports the work of the group.

1	2	3	4	5
totally disagree	disagree somewhat	not sure	agree somewhat	totally agree

Encouraging Effective Meeting Behaviors

Sometimes you'll find yourself working with groups whose members behave as though they were being paid bonuses for rudeness. People interrupt. Members run in and out. People dismiss ideas before they've really tried to understand them, and so on.

Producing outcomes is a battle in these situations. Sometimes the wisest thing to do is stop the proceedings and raise member awareness about effective meeting behaviors. This mini-training session is simple, quick, and surprisingly effective. It consists of the following steps:

1: Introduce the idea that certain behaviors are less effective than others. Hand out the sheets on the next two pages, which describe effective and ineffective meeting behaviors. Review each behavior. Answer any questions.

2: Ask all members to act as observers for the rest of the meeting. Give each person an observation sheet and ask everyone to make note of all occurrences of the listed behaviors. This means keeping track of both the names of people and the specific thing done or said.

3: At the end of the session, set aside some time to share observations.

"Were there more effective or ineffective behaviors displayed?"

"Which ineffective behaviors were in evidence?"

4: At the end of this discussion, help group members to write new norms by asking:

"What new rules should be added to the existing norms to overcome these behaviors?"

Meeting Behaviors

Behaviors that Help Effectiveness

Listens Actively	looks at the person who is speaking, nods, asks probing questions and acknowledges what is said by paraphrasing point(s) made
Supports	encourages others to develop ideas and make suggestions; gives them recognition for ideas
Probes	goes beyond surface comments by questioning teammates to uncover hidden information
Clarifies	asks members for more information about what they mean; clears up confusion
Offers Ideas	shares suggestions, ideas, solutions and proposals
Includes Others	asks quiet members for their opinions, making sure no one is left out
Summarizes	pulls together ideas from a number of people; determines where the group is and what has been covered
Harmonizes	reconciles opposing points of view; links together similar ideas; points out ideas that are the same
Manages Conflict	listens to the views of others; clarifies issues and key points made by opponents; seeks solutions

Behaviors that Hinder Effectiveness

Criticizes	makes negative comments about people/ideas
Blocks	insists on getting one's way; doesn't compromise; stands in the way of the team's progress
Grandstands	draws attention to one's personal skills; boasts
Goes off Topic	directs the conversation off onto other topics
Dominates	tries to "run" the group through dictating, bullying
Withdraws	doesn't participate or offer help/support to others
Devil's Advocate	takes pride in being contrary
"Yeah Buts"	discredits the ideas of others
Personal Slurs	hurls insults at other people

SEVEN

EFFECTIVE DECISION MAKING

Helping groups make high-quality decisions is very important but a difficult function of a facilitator. Challenges include:

o people may be trying to make a decision without having done their homework or gathering facts

o key stakeholders or decision-makers may not be present

o individuals may have a solution or position in mind that they advocate without being open to input

o people may dominate while others hold ideas back

o possible confusion about the purpose of decision-making

o conversation on whether the group is empowered to decide the issue under discussion

o missing a process to give the conversation structure, so the group engages in unstructured thrashing that's more emotional/subjective than factual/objective

o frustration causes group members to give up their quest for a solution and resort to voting or simply moving on to the next topic without closure.

Traits of effective decision making:

❏ everyone is clear about the purpose of the decision-making conversation

❏ the group knows the extent of its power to make the decision in question and the right people are present

❑ people understand the approach to be taken and are willing to follow it

❑ there is an objective and open atmosphere in which ideas are freely exchanged and considered

❑ people understand the approach and are willing to follow it

❑ all ideas are viewed as equally important and no individual or subgroup dominates

❑ if the decision process becomes deadlocked, group members stop and examine why they're stuck and seek ways of ending the impasse

❑ discussions end with a sense of closure/clear next steps.

Know the Four Types of Conversations

The first step in being able to support effective decision making is awareness that conversations fall into one of the following categories:

Information sharing—This includes giving update reports, sharing research, or brainstorming ideas for later ranking. Note that there is no decision making in these types of discussions. Information-sharing discussions are typically chaired, rather than facilitated, and result in little collaboration among participants.

Planning—These discussions feature activities such as visioning and creating goal statements, describing objectives and expected results, assessing needs, identifying priorities, and creating detailed action steps. Budget planning and program planning discussions fall into this category. Managed-change initiatives are also planning activities. Lots of decisions are made during planning conversations, thus they require structure and active facilitation to ensure input from members.

Problem solving—Encompasses activities that engage participants in identifying and resolving issues together. The core activities involve gathering data, identifying problems, analyzing the current situation, using criteria to sort potential solutions, and planning for action. Customer service initiatives and process improvement projects fall into this category. Because these types of discussions result in actions that create change, problem solving needs to be carefully structured and systematically facilitated.

Relationship building—This includes activities that help people get to know each other and build cohesion. It includes activities such as ice breakers, norm development sessions, and conflict mediations. Structured team-building sessions are an example of relationship-building discussions. Important agreements are made during relationship-building discussions, so they also need to be carefully structured and assertively facilitated.

 Always identify if the purpose of a discussion is to make decisions or simply to share information.

At the start of each conversation, facilitators must determine which of the four discussion types is taking place and whether or not the group is making decisions.

Types of Conversations	
Non-Decision	**Decision**
If it's information sharing, list making, or brainstorming	If it's planning, problem solving, or relationship building
– No decisions will be made	– Decisions will be made
– Facilitation isn't critical	– A clear process is needed
– Synergy isn't important	– Facilitation is important
– Closure is not needed	– People need to build on each other's thoughts
– Next steps are optional	– Closure and clear next steps are needed

The Four Levels of Empowerment

For all decision-making conversations, it's very important to clarify the level of empowerment at which a decision is being made and communicate that information to group members at the start of any decision-making discussion.

Nothing causes greater confusion and distrust than a lack of clarity about empowerment levels. It's very unfortunate when a group assumes that it has final say in a decision, only to discover that management was merely asking for their opinions. Fortunately, empowerment doesn't have to be a confusing concept when you use the following four-level empowerment model.

Empowerment Options			
Management Control		**Employee Control**	
I	II	III	IV
Management Decides, then Informs Staff	**Management Gets Staff Input before Deciding**	**Employees Decide & Recommend**	**Employees Decide & Act**
Telling	Selling	Participating	Delegating
Directing	Coaching	Facilitating	Liaising
Management is in control	Employees' ideas harnessed as input decisions	Accountabilities are clearly shared	Employees are accountable and responsible
Team members are told about decisions and expected to comply	Team members are consulted and have input into decisions	Team members must consult management before acting to get approval	Team members can set direction and take action without approvals

Clarifying the Four Levels of Empowerment

Level I—This refers to any decision made by management without input from employees. Employees are informed of the decision and expected to comply.

Level II—This is a decision made by management after seeking input from employees. Employees are consulted but have no actual say in the final outcome and are expected to comply. An employee focus group is an example of a Level II decision-making process.

Level III—In this category of decision, employees discuss and recommend a course of action, but are unable to act without gaining final approval. Problem-solving workshops are often set up as Level III activities.

Level IV—In this level of decision, the group has been given full authority to make a decision and implement action plans without having to seek further approvals.

It's the role of the facilitator to help group members determine the extent of their empowerment in each decision-making activity. It is best to do this during the assessment and design phases of the facilitation process, although empowerment is often clarified at the start of discussions. Clarification involves asking questions such as:

"Who's accountable for the outcomes of the decision?"

"Who is best qualified to make the decision in terms of expertise?"

"To what extent is it important that there be high levels of buy-in to the decision?"

"To what extent is it advantageous to have group members actively engaged in every step of making the decision and implementing actions?"

If you're testing a group's assumptions about the empowerment level related to a specific topic, ask:

"Is the decision being made elsewhere?" (Level I)

"Are you being asked for your recommendations?" (Level II)

"Are you making recommendations that require approval before you can act?" (Level III)

"Are you fully able to go ahead and implement whatever decision is made by the group?" (Level IV)

Adjusting Empowerment Levels

If a group feels that a decision is being made at the wrong level, facilitate a discussion about the empowerment level the members think they need. While this is often about gaining more empowerment, there are situations in which groups feel the need to reduce their level of accountability for a decision.

To raise empowerment, facilitate a discussion that asks:

"What empowerment level is appropriate for this activity?"

"Why does the group need these powers?"

"What are the risks of the group having these powers?"

"What concerns is management likely to have?"

"What checks and balances could be put into place to encourage management to empower you more?"

"What accountabilities are members prepared to assume individually and as a group to gain more power?"

Encouraging Groups to Accept Greater Empowerment

There are instances in which group members may feel that they're being asked to assume too much power. This can have a number of root causes:

○ there may be a feeling that the actions planned by the group aren't within group members' job descriptions

○ some people are unused to being empowered and are afraid to take risks

○ many people may already be overcommitted

○ there may be a lack of confidence or skill on the part of some participants

- there may be a lack of true buy-in to the action plans that were created
- there may be a justified lack of trust that the organization is going to support the group's initiatives.

To explore the need to reduce empowerment, facilitate a discussion that asks:

"What power/authority is appropriate for this activity?"

"Why should the empowerment level be lower?"

"What accountabilities are group members unprepared to assume?"

"What risks should management be made aware of?"

There are situations in which group members shy away from assuming greater responsibility when they shouldn't. A common example is groups in which members enjoy analyzing a problem and brainstorming solutions, but back away from taking responsibility for action.

Unlike managers, who may have the authority to "order" reluctant employees to take on new tasks, facilitators have to rely on their process skills to encourage people to overcome resistance. If you encounter unjustified resistance to empowerment, you can take the following actions:

1. Acknowledge the resistance—Don't ignore or deny it:

   "I can tell by your reaction that you don't want to take on responsibility for this decision/program."

2. Invite members to verbalize their reticence—Allow people to vent their fears and concerns:

   "Why do you think responsibility should rest elsewhere?"

3. Empathize with their situation—Sympathize without agreeing:

   "I can understand that you're concerned about taking on more responsibility at this time."

4. Engage members in identifying strategies—Ask them to identify conditions for overcoming their resistance:

"Under what conditions would you consider assuming more responsibility?" or *"What assurances, training, or support would make you feel you'd be willing to give it a try?"*

5. **Paraphrase and summarize their statements—** Encourage them to agree to greater empowerment by ratifying their suggestions:

"So you're saying that you'd be willing to take this on with some training and coaching."

In most situations, group members will identify feasible and realistic things that can be done to encourage them to buy-in further. If, on the other hand, group members state unreasonable conditions, such as having their pay doubled, don't react. Record all unreasonable ideas along with the others until the list of conditions is complete. Then ask the group to help review the list of conditions to identify which are feasible and which are unrealistic. In most cases, other group members will edit out the more outrageous demands of their peers.

 Facilitators may need to help groups work through their resistance to increased empowerment.

Does this approach always work? The truth is that nothing works in every situation. It is, however, the only process tool available given the facilitator's lack of true power over the group. If this approach fails to work, you will have to refer the problem of group reluctance to assume accountability to the leader, who will decide whether ordering increased empowerment is the best course of action.

Be aware that bringing in leaders to order members to take on more empowerment will result in reduced buy-in and may also regress the group's maturity.

To avoid these negatives, always try to engage members in conversations aimed at overcoming their resistance first.

Shifting Decision-Making Paradigms

All facilitators need to be aware that when organizations start involving groups to make decisions that were formerly made solely by management, this may represent a major shift in the cultural values of the organization.

Many managers are used to listening to input and then making important decisions themselves. Such patterns are a reality that all facilitators have to understand. When staff input into decision making represents a major change to traditional power arrangements, you must help leaders and members appreciate the value of participative decisions and create the right setting in which people can be encouraged to express their ideas freely.

When working with a group you don't know, never assume that participative decision making is understood or practiced by either the group or the leader. Instead, check by asking questions that probe how the organization normally makes decisions. Ask things like:

"How are decisions of this nature typically made in this organization?"

"To what extent are employees used to making these types of decisions?"

"Are member decisions often overturned by leaders?"

In addition, leaders who are accustomed to a directive style may have concerns about relinquishing control. These leaders often need time to buy into the idea of participation in decision making. They also need to understand how this greater employee involvement benefits them. Some points that may be helpful in encouraging a leader to accept increased group decision-making empowerment include:

○ group decision making has the benefit of generating more ideas, building commitment, and encouraging members to take greater responsibility

- group decision making relieves the leader of many tasks and frees him or her to play more strategic roles in the organization

- decisions that involve a degree of risk can be managed at Level III empowerment to ensure that the leader approves member decisions before they are implemented

- decisions that members are fully empowered to make at Level IV can be given clear parameters to ensure they meet key success criteria, such as: compliance with budgetary guidelines, support of the overall strategic plan, etc.

While facilitators often lead decision-making sessions at Level II, it should always be made clear to leaders that this isn't the full use of a group's powers. Years of experience has shown that decision making at Levels III and IV more fully taps into the talents and resources of group members and creates a more fully engaged organization.

The Decision-Making Options

Whenever you need to help a group make a decision, you can use one of five distinct decision-making methods. Each of these options represents a different approach. Each has pros and cons. A decision option should always be chosen carefully to be sure it fits. Examples showing exactly how to use these approaches are provided throughout Chapter Four of this book. In each Structured Conversation, you will be given guidance about when and how to use the five decision options described below.

The Five Decision Options

- Building a **consensus** through joint analysis and brainstorming

- Making lists and then using **multi-voting** to prioritize options

- Building a **compromise** option to bridge the gap between two positions

- Using **majority voting** to decide between competing options
- **One person** makes a decision that's binding on the group

Consensus Building

 Consensus building creates participation and buy-in to the generated solutions.

Consensus building means ensuring that everyone has a clear understanding of the situation or issue to be decided, analyzing all of the relevant facts together and then jointly developing solutions that represent the whole group's best thinking about the optimal decision. Consensus building is characterized by a lot of listening, healthy debate and testing of options. Consensus generates a decision about which everyone says:

"I can live with it."

Pros—It's a collaborative effort that unites the group. It demands high involvement. It's systematic, objective and fact-driven. It builds buy-in and high commitment to the outcome.

Cons—It's time-consuming and produces low-quality decisions if done without proper data collection or if the wrong people are in the room.

Uses—When a decision will impact the entire group, when buy-in and ideas from all members are essential and/or when the importance of the decision being made is worth the time it will take to complete the consensus process.

Steps—Name the issue, topic or problem. Share all of the known facts to create a shared understanding of the current situation. Generate potential courses of action/solutions. Generate criteria for sorting the courses of action/solutions. Use the criteria to sort the ideas (can be a decision grid, vote or multi-vote). Make a clear statement of decision. Ratify that all can live with the solution.

Multi-Voting

 Multi-voting is a kind of voting activity that's useful when there are a lot of options or a lot of people involved.

Multi-voting is a priority-setting tool that's useful for making decisions when the group has a lengthy set of options. Rank ordering the options, based on a set of criteria, will clarify the best course of action.

Pros—it's systematic, objective, democratic, noncompetitive and participative. Everyone wins somewhat, and feelings of loss are minimal. It's a fast way of sorting out a complex set of options. Often feels consensual.

Cons—it's often associated with limited discussion, hence, limited understanding of the options. It also may force choices on people that may not be satisfactory to them, when the real priorities do not rise to the surface. Sometimes people are swayed by each other if the voting is done out in the open, rather than electronically or by secret ballot.

Uses—when there's a long list of alternatives or items to choose from.

Steps—After the group has generated a wide range of solutions, clarify the criteria that define the votes (most important, easiest, least expensive, greatest impact, etc.). If using stickers, hand out strips of dots. If using markers, tell people how many marks to make. If using points, clarify how many points people can distribute (10/100, etc.) Allow people to mill as they affix their votes.

Compromise

 Compromise involves finding a middle position between two opposing options.

Compromise is a negotiated approach that's applicable when there are two or more distinct options and members are strongly polarized (neither side is willing to accept the solution or position put forth by the other side). A middle position is then created that incorporates ideas from both sides. Throughout the process of negotiation, everyone wins a few points, but they also lose favored items. The outcome, therefore, is something that no one is totally satisfied with. In compromises, no one feels they got exactly what they wanted, so the emotional reaction is often, "It's not really what I wanted, but I'm going to have to live with it."

Pros—It generates lots of discussion, and does create a solution.

Cons—Negotiating when people are pushing a favored point of view tends to be adversarial, hence this approach divides the group. In the end, everyone wins, but everyone also loses.

Uses—When two opposing solutions are proposed, neither of which is acceptable to everyone; or when the group is strongly polarized and compromise is the only alternative.

Steps—Invite the two parties to give a description of the solution or course of action that they favor. Ask one party to make notes and then give a short summary of the solution or position favored by the other group. Engage the entire group in identifying the strengths and weaknesses of each proposed approach. Bring forward the strengths of both approaches. Create a third option or hybrid that builds on the strengths of both positions. Ask each group to willingly give up some aspects of their original approach in order to arrive at a decision that represents a middle ground. Clarify, summarize and ratify the middle-ground approach.

Majority Voting

This involves asking people to choose the option they favor, once clear choices have been identified. Usual methods are a show of hands or secret ballot. The quality of voting is always enhanced if there's good discussion to share ideas before a vote is taken.

 The quality of any voting exercise increases dramatically if it's preceded by a thorough discussion.

Pros—It's fast, and decisions can be high quality if the vote is preceded by a thorough analysis.

Cons—It can be too fast, and low in quality if people vote based on their personal feelings, without the benefit of hearing each other's thoughts or facts. It creates winners and losers, hence dividing the group. The show of hands method may put pressure on people to conform.

Uses—When there are two distinct options, a decision must be made quickly and a division in the group is acceptable. Use it mostly to make trivial decisions or to take the pulse of the group.

Steps—Ask members to describe both options in some details to build a shared understanding. Identify criteria for deciding which is more effective (timeliness, cost, impact, etc.). Once everyone understands both options and the criteria for deciding, use a show of hands or paper vote to identify which option to implement.

There are no examples of majority voting in Chapter Four of this book because it is not the optimal way to help a group reach a decision since it causes division.

One Person Decides

This is a decision that the group decides to empower one person to make on behalf of the group. A common misconception among teams is that every decision needs to be made by the whole group. In some situations, a one-person decision is not only faster, but a more effective way to get resolution. The quality of any one-person decision will be raised considerably if the person making the decision gets input from group members before deciding.

 Many groups ignore the fact that many decisions are best made by one person.

Pros—It's fast and accountability is clear. Can result in commitment and buy-in if people feel their ideas are represented.

Cons—It can divide the group if the person deciding doesn't consult the group or makes a decision that others can't live with. A one-person decision typically lacks in both the buy-in and synergy that come from a group decision-making process.

Uses—When there's a clear expert in the group; when only one person has the information needed to make the decision and can't share it; or when one person is solely accountable for the outcome when the issue is unimportant or small.

Steps—Identify the expert who's best qualified to make the decision. To build buy-in, conduct a consultation during which group members tell the expert about their needs and concerns regarding the item to be decided. Gain agreement that everyone will accept the decision of the expert.

 Each option has its place, so choose the most appropriate method for each decision-making session.

Decision Options

Options	Pros	Cons	Uses
Consensus Building	Collaborative, systematic, participative, discussion-oriented, encourages commitment	Takes time, requires data and member skills	Important issues, when total buy-in matters
Multi-Voting	Systematic, objective, participative, feels like a win	Limits dialogue, influenced choices, real priorities may not surface	To sort or prioritize a long list of options
Compromise	Discussion, creates a solution	Adversarial, win/lose, divides the group	When positions are polarized, when consensus is improbable
Majority Voting	Fast, high quality with dialogue, clear outcome	May be too fast, winners and losers, influenced choices, lack of input	Trivial matter, if division of group is acceptable
One Person Decides	Can be fast, clear accountability	Lack of input, low buy-in, no synergy	When one person is the expert, individual willing to take sole responsibility

The Importance of Building Consensus

The crucial importance of building consensus simply cannot be overstated and must be fully understood by all facilitators. In fact, facilitation and consensus building are based on the same set of core values and beliefs.

Besides being the number-one choice for making all important decisions, facilitators always seek to build consensus with everything they do. Consensus activities include:

o summarizing a complex set of ideas to the satisfaction of group members

o gaining buy-in for all the purposes/goals of a session

o obtaining everyone's input about clear goals/objectives

o linking thoughts together so people can formulate a common idea

o making notes on a flip chart in such a way that each member feels he or she has been heard and is satisfied with what's been recorded

Because all facilitation activities must strive to be collaborative, participative, synergistic, and unifying, they are essentially consensus building in nature!

Hallmarks of the Consensus Process

Regardless of whether a multi-step process is being used to build a decision or the facilitator is only synthesizing group thoughts into a consensus statement, the same hallmarks of the process are always present:

o lots of ideas are shared

o everyone's ideas are heard

o active listening and paraphrasing to clarify ideas

o people build on each other's ideas

o no pushing a pre-determined solution; instead, there's an open and objective quest for new options

- the final solution is based on sound information

- when the final solution is reached, people feel satisfied that they were part of the decision

- all feel so consulted and involved that even though the final solution isn't the one they would have chosen working on their own, they can readily "live with it."

There are many situations in which the decisions to be made are so important that consensus is the only acceptable method. Defaulting to voting or any other technique that creates division within the group allows dissenters to absolve themselves of responsibility for important group outcomes. In these cases, the group must agree to keep discussing the issue until everyone indicates that he or she can live with the outcome.

It is also important never to end a consensus exercise by asking whether everyone is happy or everyone agrees with the outcome. Consensus is not about either happiness of total agreement. At the end of even a great consensus process, people have usually made concessions and are usually not getting everything they wanted.

Don't ask: *"Do we all agree?"* or *"Is everyone happy?"*

Instead ask: *"Do we have a well-thought-through outcome that we can all feel committed to implementing and that everyone can live with?"*

One of the major contributions of any facilitator is in helping a group overcome the temptation to "pressure" dissenters into agreement. By openly accepting and discussing differences, facilitators help members reach decisions that have been objectively explored and tested.

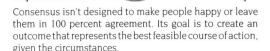

Consensus isn't designed to make people happy or leave them in 100 percent agreement. Its goal is to create an outcome that represents the best feasible course of action, given the circumstances.

Overcoming Blocks to Consensus

It's very common that some group members may be reluctant to support a particular decision. In these cases never yield to the temptation to pressure dissenters to give in. To do so would be to court "group think."

Instead, reframe dissenters as people who may potentially have an important idea overlooked by the group. This involves acknowledging and accepting the dissent, then harnessing it to improve the decision. This is done by allowing the dissenters to express their concerns in really concrete terms and then making them accountable for finding solutions to the issues that they raise.

> *"Tell us the specific issue that you have with the group's decision. What do you see as the flaws in this decision? What's been overlooked?"*

> *"What changes do you propose could be made to the group's solution that would make it acceptable to you? What are the solutions to the problems that you raise?"*

Things to Watch for in Decision Making

❑ Be clear upfront on the process/tools to be used.

❑ Ask people what assumptions they're operating under, either about the issue or the organizational constraints. *Note these and test them with the rest of the group.*

❑ Always confront natural conflict differences assertively and collaboratively. Don't strive to avoid conflict or accommodate by asking people to be nice and get along.

❑ Urge people not to fold or just give in if they feel they have important ideas. When everyone agrees just to make things run smoothly, the result is "group think."

This creates poor decisions made just to get it over with and ensure that everyone stays friends.

❏ If the group has chosen to go for consensus because the issue is important, stick with it, even if the going gets tough. No voting, coin tossing or bargaining.

❏ Be very particular about achieving closure and consensus on any items that are decided.

❏ Stop the action if things start "spinning" or behaviors are ineffective. **Ask:** *"What are we doing well? What aren't we doing so well?"* and *"What do we need to do about it?"* Then act on all suggestions.

Effective Decision-Making Behaviors

To make any decision process work, group members need to behave in specific ways. These behaviors can be suggested to the group or generated as norms in advance of any decision-making session. Sharing the chart below may help encourage effective behaviors.

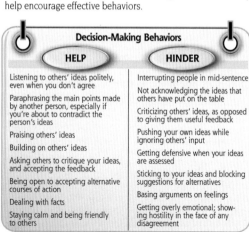

| Decision-Making Behaviors | |
HELP	HINDER
Listening to others' ideas politely, even when you don't agree	Interrupting people in mid-sentence
Paraphrasing the main points made by another person, especially if you're about to contradict the person's ideas	Not acknowledging the ideas that others have put on the table
Praising others' ideas	Criticizing others' ideas, as opposed to giving them useful feedback
Building on others' ideas	Pushing your own ideas while ignoring others' input
Asking others to critique your ideas, and accepting the feedback	Getting defensive when your ideas are assessed
Being open to accepting alternative courses of action	Sticking to your ideas and blocking suggestions for alternatives
Dealing with facts	Basing arguments on feelings
Staying calm and being friendly to others	Getting overly emotional; showing hostility in the face of any disagreement

Symptoms, Causes, and Cures of Poor Decisions

When groups make poor-quality decisions, one or more of the following symptoms may be in evidence:

Symptom 1: *Aimless drifting and random discussions. The same topic is kicked around meeting after meeting without resolution. It feels like the group is spinning its wheels.*

Cause: No plan or process for approaching the decision. Group members simply launch into the discussion without any thought to which tools to use. Without a systematic approach, people start proposing solutions before there has been a thorough analysis of the situation. There is a lack of proper information. Everyone puts his or her favorite solution on the table. No one takes notes. No solution is ever definitively agreed to. Detailed action plans aren't written down.

Cure: The group needs a structured approach to decision making that uses the right decision-making tool and is assertively facilitated.

Symptom 2: *The group uses voting on important items where total buy-in is important, then uses consensus to decide trivia.*

Cause: A lack of understanding of decision-making options. The group doesn't understand the six key decision-making options and when to use each of them.

Cure: The group needs to become familiar with the six main decision-making options and consciously decide which to use before any decision-making discussions.

Symptom 3: *The group always seems to run out of time just when the important decisions are on the table.*

Cause: Poor time management. Time isn't budgeted or monitored. There's no detailed agenda that sets aside sufficient time to deal with important items. Hence, time is wasted discussing less important aspects. Meetings often start late or run over.

Cure: The group needs to create a detailed agenda before each meeting. During discussions, the facilitator must be assertive about keeping the group on track and on time.

Symptom 4: *When an important item is on the table, people grow heated and argumentative. No one really listens to the opposing viewpoints. Everyone pushes his or her point in an attempt to "win." Some members dominate, unconcerned that others are silent.*

Cause: Poorly developed group interaction skills. People have become positional and competitive. No one is listening to the points other people are making, just pushing his or her own. Facilitation is nonexistent or weak. As a result, there's an absence of the synergy that exists when people build on each other's ideas. This confrontational style strains relationships, which only makes things worse.

Cure: The members need training in group effectiveness skills so that they can exhibit more listening, supporting, and idea building. If a facilitator is present, he or she should stop the conversation and explain active listening and paraphrasing. When conversation resumes, the facilitator should ensure that people are acknowledging each other's points.

Symptom 5: *After a lengthy discussion, it becomes clear that everyone is operating on slightly different assumptions about the problem and what the constraints/possibilities are.*

Cause: Failure to check assumptions. Everyone has a different view of the situation and is basing his or her input on that view. Assumptions are never put on the table for sharing or testing.

Cure: Use probing questions to uncover the assumptions underlying statements made by the members. These questions can be related to the situation, the organization, or the people involved. Once assumptions are clarified and validated, members will be operating in the same framework.

Symptom 6: *In spite of the fact that the discussion has been going in circles for some time, no one takes action to get things back on track.*

Cause: No process checking. Even when things are going nowhere and frustration levels are running high, no one knows to call time-out to take stock and regroup. This, once again, reflects the absence of facilitation.

Cure: Stopping the discussion periodically to ask how things are going, whether the pace is right, whether people feel progress is being made, and whether people feel the right approach is being taken. (Refer to the discussion of process checking in Chapter One.)

ONE OF
THE MOST
IMPORTANT
ROLES OF A
FACILITATOR
IS TO HELP
GROUPS MAKE
COMPLEX
DECISIONS.

Chapter EIGHT

FACILITATING CONFLICT

Dealing with conflict is a fact of every facilitator's life. For starters, remember that differences of opinion are a normal part of any human interaction, so relax. The fact that people are arguing does not mean that you're doing a poor job. It is, however, a call to action. As facilitators, we need to intervene to restore group effectiveness. Standing on the sidelines is simply not an option.

Your actions can determine whether people debate or argue.

Comparing Arguments and Debates

Understanding the differences between a debate and an argument is critical. Healthy debate is essential—if a group doesn't express differences of opinion, then it's basically incapable of making effective decisions. Dysfunctional arguments, on the other hand, lead to disaster. Facilitators don't limit debate; they keep it from becoming dysfunctional.

Accept that differences of opinion are normal and that you need to play an active role to restore group effectiveness.

Comparing Debates and Arguments

Debates

People are open to hearing others' ideas.

People listen and respond to ideas even if they don't agree with them.

Everyone tries to understand the views of others.

People stay objective and focus on the facts.

There's a systematic approach to analyzing the situation and looking for solutions.

Arguments

People assume they're right.

People wait until others have finished talking, then state their ideas without responding to the ideas of others.

No one is interested in how others see the situation.

People get personally attacked and blamed.

Hot topics get thrashed out in an unstructured way.

Repairs it

Stay totally neutral

Point out differences so they can be understood

Insist that people listen politely—have rules and use them

Make people paraphrase each other's ideas

Ask for concerns

Make people focus on facts

Problem-solve concerns

Invite and face feedback

Facilitate assertively

Get closure and move on

Keeps it going

Join the argument

Ignore differences—just pray that they will go away

Let people be rude—set no norms

Ignore the fact that no one is really hearing anyone else

Sidestep hot issues

Let people get personal

Get defensive

Squash dissent

Stand by passively

Let it drag on and on

Here's an important tip: Even though we write about conflict, never say the actual word "conflict" in a group setting, even if that word accurately describes what's going on. The word "conflict" is loaded with meaning. It also makes differences seem more serious and could make matters worse.

Instead, use language that downplays what's going on. Instead of saying: *"It seems that you two are having a conflict,"* substitute *"It seems that there are differing views on this subject. Let's stop and make sure these points of view are heard and understood."* This less-inflammatory language helps make differences look like a normal exchange.

 Instead of labeling something as a conflict, call it differing views.

Steps in Managing Conflict

One of the most helpful things to know about managing conflict is that it needs to be handled in two separate and distinct chronological steps:

1: **Venting**—This involves listening to people so that they feel heard and so that their built-up emotions are diffused. People are rarely ready to move on to solutions until they have had the opportunity to fully vent their feelings.

2: **Resolving the issue**—When it appears that feelings have been expressed and all differing views have been heard and acknowledged, help members resolve the issues. This involves taking a structured approach to help group members reach solutions. Resolution can come through a collaborative problem-solving activity, helping members create an acceptable compromise, or supporting some members in accommodating or consciously avoiding the topic temporarily to allow time for emotions to further cool. Let's look at these steps in detail.

Step 7 : Venting Emotions

Facilitators need to vent emotions when they see:

o people are pushing their points of view without being at all receptive to the ideas of others

o people are becoming angry, defensive, and personal

o there's negative body language, for example, glaring/pointing

o sarcastic or dismissive remarks are made

o people "yeah but" and criticize each other's ideas

o some people shut down and withdraw

o there's extreme anger.

 In conflicts you need to facilitate calmly, yet assertively!

When negative emotions are in evidence, facilitators need to act quickly so that these feelings don't poison the dynamics of the group. To vent conflict:

o **Slow things down**—Get the attention of members by stopping the action and asking to slow down. Use the excuse that you can't take notes that quickly. Ask speakers to start over and repeat key ideas.

o **Stay totally neutral**—Never take sides or allow your body language to hint that you favor certain ideas.

o **Watch your language**—Don't use loaded words like **arguing, conflict,** or **anger.**

o **Stay calm**—Maintain your composure and do not raise your own voice. Speak slowly with an even tone. Avoid using emotional body language.

o **Emphasize listening**—Paraphrase key points and ask others to tell the group what they are hearing.

o **Revisit the norms**—Point out the existing norms and remind people of their prior agreements. Ask people to tell you the difference between a healthy debate and an argument. Ask them which they are interested in having. Have them tell you the rules of a healthy debate. Add these new norms to the existing norm set.

o **Be assertive**—Move into referee mode. Insist that people speak one at a time. Stop interruptions. Don't stand by passively while people become emotional.

o **Make interventions**—Don't ignore ineffective or dysfunctional behaviors. Refer to the Making Interventions section later in this chapter for the appropriate wording for making interventions that redirect behavior.

o **Record key ideas**—Make notes about key points to keep them from getting lost and to stop group members from repeating points. Read these notes back to the group whenever you want to regain control.

o **Seek permission to move on**—Ask members whether they feel that their points of view have been heard and acknowledged. Also ask whether they are ready to move on to resolve the matter.

 When dealing with a group that is deeply locked in conflict, it may be helpful to hand out a sheet that features the LECSR model that follows.

Listen-Empathize-Clarify-Seek Permission-Resolve

1. **Listen**—Instead of arguing when you hear a point you disagree with, listen attentively to the other person's main points. Let people share their views without interruption. Look interested and say things like:

   "Tell me more. That's interesting. Uh-huh."

   "I'm not sure I understand. Could you go over that again?"

2. **Empathize**—Accept the views of the other person even if you don't agree with them. Let people know you understand their feelings. Say:

"I don't blame you for feeling that way. I see what you mean."

"I understand how you feel. I'm sure I'd feel the same way if. . . ."

3. **Clarify**—Delve deeper to ensure that you have a clear understanding of what the other is saying to you. Say:

"Let me see if I have it straight; what you're saying is. . . ."

"Is it possible that. . . . The idea you're proposing is. . . ."

4. **Seek Permission**—Tell your side after the other person has expressed his or her concerns and feels clearly understood. Say: *"Now that I understand your views, can I explain mine?"* or *"It seems that this would be a good time to bring up a few points you haven't mentioned."*

5. **Resolve the Issue**—Once you have both heard each other, start dealing with the problem together.

Step 2: Resolving Issues

Once emotions are vented and acknowledged, there are five basic approaches to address the underlying issue:

Avoid	Offer members the option of placing the issue in the parking lot for later.
Accommodate	Ask people to be more tolerant and accept each other's views.
Compromise	Look for middle ground between highly polarized views. Ask each person to give up some less important items.
Compete	This is a form of conflict resolution in which people debate until one party wins. Results in a win/lose.
Collaborate	Face the conflict, draw people's attention to it, surface the issues, and resolve them in a win/win by using systematic problem solving.

The Five Conflict Options: Pros and Cons

Each of the aforementioned approaches can work in specific situations. Facilitators need to understand each one and choose the one that suits the situation.

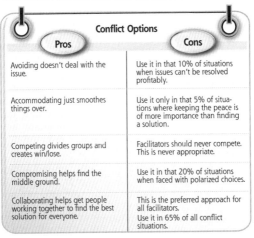

Conflict Options	
Pros	**Cons**
Avoiding doesn't deal with the issue.	Use it in that 10% of situations when issues can't be resolved profitably.
Accommodating just smooths things over.	Use it only in that 5% of situations where keeping the peace is of more importance than finding a solution.
Competing divides groups and creates win/lose.	Facilitators should never compete. This is never appropriate.
Compromising helps find the middle ground.	Use it in that 20% of situations when faced with polarized choices.
Collaborating helps get people working together to find the best solution for everyone.	This is the preferred approach for all facilitators. Use it in 65% of all conflict situations.

Collaboration encourages people to work together to objectively seek solutions that they can all live with. Because it's consensual, it unites and generates solutions that everyone feels committed to implementing.

People listen actively and build on each other's points. Solutions are generated through the use of non-competitive processes such as brainstorming. The best course of action is determined by applying a set of criteria to the choices available.

Collaborating is the superior conflict option!

Preventing Conflict

In the same way that an ounce of prevention is worth a pound of cure, it's always best to create an environment where conflict is less likely to happen in the first place. One way to do this is to engage the groups you work with in setting rules that define how people ought to interact.

In behavioral science terms this is known as setting norms. Norms are rules or guidelines that describe how people will behave or how things will get done. These rules can be created anytime a problem occurs, but are more powerful when created to head off problems before they crop up.

You can use *Norming* to prevent conflict by helping a group create rules of conduct. This is especially powerful when you engage people in setting rules for situations that are anticipated to cause problems in the future. Used in this way, *Norming* becomes a preventive strategy.

Simply setting rules doesn't guarantee harmony, but at least they provide a starting point. The process is easy. Rules or guidelines can be created at a meeting or before groups ever meet via email. Whether the rules are created in a face-to-face conversation or at a distance, the process is always the same: You simply ask specific *Norming* questions and then ratify the answers that people provide. Examples of *Norming* questions can be found on the next page.

Norming is also an important tool to use after a conflict or problem has occurred. In this setting ask members to suggest rules that will help to ensure that a similar type of incident will never happen again.

When a group has a clear set of rules, anyone can point out if a rule is being ignored. This shares responsibility for maintaining a healthy climate.

Facilitation at a Glance! | Fourth Edition | ©2018 GOAL/QPC

Norming is extremely simple, but don't let its simplicity fool you. A set of rules that everyone has agreed to honor is a powerful tool for preventing strife. Below are some examples of Norming questions for a variety of situations. Notice that the person posing the questions is asking very detailed questions aimed at eliciting specific and clear rules.

Norming Questions to Generate Rules for Effective Meetings

"What can we do, at all our meetings, to ensure that we always have healthy debates instead of heated arguments? What specific behaviors would help?"

"What should we do anytime a conversation gets stuck and we start spinning in nonproductive circles?"

"What is it okay for any one of us to say if someone's presentation goes on for too long?"

"What rule do you want to have about side-chatting during meetings?"

"What should the rule be about coming and going during meetings?"

"What should the rule be about texting and working on laptops while we're discussing an agenda item?"

"What is it okay for any of us to say if we notice someone breaking one of these rules during a meeting?"

Making Interventions

During any workshop or meeting, there may be occasions when the facilitator will need to make an intervention. The definition of an intervention is any action or set of actions deliberately taken to improve the functioning of the group. This may be necessary in situations in which:

- two people are having a side conversation
- people are interrupting and not listening to each other
- people become overly emotional
- the discussion is stuck or off track.

Intervening is like holding up a mirror to the participants so that they can see what they're doing and take steps to correct the problem. Regardless of its length and complexity, an intervention is always an interruption. You're stopping the discussion about the task to draw member attention to an aspect of the process. Since this constitutes an interruption in the flow of discussion, it should be done as quickly as possible so that members can return to the task.

The need to intervene may arise because of one individual, two people, or the whole group. Groups commonly experience problems that involve all of the members, such as when everyone is looking at their handheld devices and not paying attention to the discussion or when people become tired and zone out.

Facilitators need to be cautious about whether or not to intervene. If you intervened every single time there was a problem, you could be interrupting too frequently. Instead, keep a watchful eye for repetitive, inappropriate behaviors that aren't resolving themselves. Those are the ones that deserve an intervention.

You're obligated to take action if the group's effectiveness declines.

Deciding Whether to Intervene

- Is the problem serious?
- Do we have enough time to cause a disruption?
- How will it impact relationships and meeting flow?
- Can the intervention hurt the climate or the self-esteem of participants?
- What's the chance that the intervention will work?
- Do I know these people well enough to do this?
- Do I have enough credibility to do this?
- Is it appropriate given their level of openness/trust?

Wording an Intervention

Interventions are always risky because they can make the situation worse. For this reason, interventions need to be carefully worded. There are three distinct wording components to an intervention:

Statement 1: Describe what you see. This is non-judgmental and doesn't attribute motive. It's based solely on observations of actual events. Example: *"I'm noticing that we're now on a topic that's not on our agenda."*

Statement 2: Make an impact statement. Tell members how their actions are impacting you, the process, or other people. Base this on actual observations. Example: *"I'm concerned that you aren't going to get to your other topics."*

Statement 3: Redirect ineffective behavior(s). This can be done by:

(a) **Asking** members for their suggestions. Example: *"What do we need to do to get back to our agenda?"*

(b) **Telling** members what to do. Example: *"Would you please end this conversation so we can get back on track?"*

Statement 1: Takes a snapshot to create awareness of an ineffective situation. Statement 1 does not resolve the situation, but is important to set the stage for the rest of the intervention.

Statement 2: Expresses a concern that serves as a rationale for making the intervention. Impact statements are best when they express concern for the person at whom the intervention is aimed. Impact statements can be omitted from an intervention if they seem to lay blame or worsen the situation in any way. Like Statement 1, impact statements do not resolve the situation.

Statement 3: Redirects the situation and is the most important element in an intervention. Statement 3 resolves the situation. It can be in the form of tactfully telling/asking people for suggestions to improve the situation.

An intervention can be made using all three statements, Statements 1 and 3, Statements 2 and 3, or Statement 3 on its own. The bottom line is that Statement 3, the redirect, is always necessary.

 Choose the right language to intervene; don't assume or judge!

Telling vs. Asking

When making an intervention, remember the following rules:

- Asking is always better than telling because people are more likely to accept their own interventions

- The more a group acts maturely and responsibly, the more effective it is to ask rather than tell

- A directive or telling intervention is appropriate if individuals are exhibiting dysfunctional or low-maturity behavior. In these cases, asking will not elicit an effective response.

Wording for Specific Situations

Use extremely tactful language that doesn't sound critical. The examples below are all very tactfully worded to sound supportive rather than punitive. Don't be overwhelmed by this technique. It may seem difficult, but there are really only a handful of dysfunctions that routinely occur. Simply write out the likely situations and create the three sentences that you will use and memorize them.

When two people are side-chatting: *"Alan. Sue. I see you having a discussion. I'm concerned that we're no longer benefitting from your ideas. We need you back."*

When people run in and out of a meeting: *"I've noticed several people coming and going. I'm concerned this may be disrupting the flow. What should we do?"*

When one person dominates the discussion: *"Joe, I'm noticing that you've already shared a lot of ideas. I'm concerned that you're not going to get to hear anyone else's report. Please wrap up with a summary of the most important ideas that you have shared so far."*

When two people are arguing and not listening to each other: *"I'm noticing that you're each repeating your points. I'm concerned that you may not be hearing each other's ideas. I'm going to ask you both to first paraphrase what the other has said before you make your own comment."*

When members are disregarding their own norms: *"I'm noticing that you're ignoring some of your rules. So let's stop and look at the norms we set last week. What do we need to do to ensure they're being followed?"*

When the meeting has totally digressed: *"I'd like to point out that you're now discussing a topic that isn't on the agenda. I'm concerned that you aren't going to get to your other topics. Do you want to continue discussing this topic or should we park it?"*

When someone is being sarcastic: *"Ellen, I'm concerned that your ideas aren't being heard because of the tone of voice you're using. Please make your point again, only in a more neutral way."*

When one person is putting down the ideas of another: *"Joe, you've been listing the cons of Carol's ideas. I'm concerned that we haven't tapped into your expertise. Please tell Carol what you think the pros of her idea are or offer her some suggestions to improve her idea."*

When someone hurls a personal slur at someone else: *"Jim, rather than characterizing Sally as being sloppy, please tell her specifically about the state of the meeting room after her session, so that she can address the situation."*

When the meeting has stalled: *"I'm noticing that I haven't written anything for a while. I'm concerned the meeting may be stalled. What can we do to get things going again?"*

When the whole group looks exhausted: *"I'm noticing that people are slumped in their seats and that we're not making much progress. Tell me what this means and what should we do about it."*

Norm-Based Interventions

One of the reasons for creating a set of norms is that these can be used to manage ineffective behaviors. When group members break one of the rules that they set themselves, the norm can be used as the basis for the intervention.

Here are some examples:

When people run in and out: *"I'm noticing that several people have left the meeting this hour. I'm concerned that you're breaking a rule you set earlier. Please remember your commitment not to come and go during the meeting."*

When people talk over each other: *"I'm concerned that you're breaking your own rule about only one conversation at a time. Please remember that you agreed to listen actively and not interrupt while others were speaking."*

When people get out their laptops and handhelds: *"I'm noticing that several people are texting. You're ignoring the rule you set earlier about this. Please hold off until the break."*

 Silence is okay. Use it to break the tempo of a conflict and to give people a chance to catch their breath.

Body Language Interventions

People constantly communicate nonverbally. They will do things like fold their arms, roll their eyes, or look puzzled. Facilitators intervene about nonverbal communication to help people express what they're projecting.

Body language interventions follow a two-step formula that is a variation of the three-step model already described. Here is that variation:

Step *1* : Describe what you see.

Step *2*: Ask what it means and offer options.

Here are some examples:

"I see a frown. What does that mean? Have we missed a point or is there something you don't agree with?"

"I'm noticing some yawns. Tell me what that means. Do we need a break or should we pick up the pace?"

"I see a puzzled look. Tell me what that means. Are you clear about what is being discussed or has someone made a point you need to hear more about?"

Making interventions is not easy, but it is essential! Facilitators simply cannot stand by while ineffective behaviors persist. The key is to master the language of interventions so your comments are supportive and helpful rather than critical or punitive!

 It may be advantageous to make some interventions in private, but you can't call a break each time you need to intervene!

Dealing with Resistance

It is a fact of life in today's busy workplace that people may be stressed by demanding workloads. In these situations they may resist the idea of taking part in any activities that could add to their workloads. Facilitators always have to be aware of this and be prepared with a strategy for dealing with both open and hidden resistance.

Reasons for resistance to your facilitation efforts:

○ the timing or location of the meeting might be poor

○ participants may have insufficient meeting notice

○ the topic of the meeting may not reflect the participants' needs

○ people may worry that the session will result in additional work

○ they may suspect that nothing will happen as a result of the meeting

○ they may fear the organization won't support their ideas.

Sometimes this resistance comes out in the open when an outspoken member speaks up and vents a concern. At other times it remains hidden, expressed only in people's negative body language or lack of participation.

The Wrong Way to Manage Resistance

When faced with resistance the worst course of action for facilitators is to become defensive or look for ways to simply push through. On the surface, this may seem to work, but compliance does not build buy-in or commitment.

Facilitators need to resist the temptation to meet force with force and instead use the facilitation tools on the next page to manage resistance in meetings.

 Using telling or selling to deal with resistance never works when you have no power or control over it.

The Right Approach

In using the correct approach, the facilitator adheres to a consistent process. The correct approach for dealing with resistance consists of two steps:

1: **Venting the concerns.** You invite the resister to express his or her resistance while you listen actively, paraphrase, and offer empathy. No matter what he or she says or how he says it, you stay calm and act totally supportive of the resister. You say things like:

"Tell me why you feel this way."

"What happened last time?"

"What went wrong?"

"Why did it happen?"

"How did you feel?"

"What were the consequences for you?"

2: **Resolving blocks and barriers.** After the concerns have been acknowledged, you ask questions to prompt the resister to suggest solutions to the barriers. This questioning is intentionally detailed and complex so that the resister has to stop and think. It centers on questions like:

"What circumstances would make you willing to stay?"

"What assurances would eliminate your concerns?"

"What supports would enable you to continue?"

"What can we do to make this work for you?"

Why this Approach Works

Taking a facilitative or questioning approach works because the resister is allowed to vent his or her frustration and be heard. The person is then consulted about what to do next. Since people don't generally refuse to act on their own suggestions, most people will abandon their resistance and move forward.

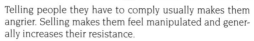

Telling people they have to comply usually makes them angrier. Selling makes them feel manipulated and generally increases their resistance.

Every day, meeting leaders handle resistance incorrectly by telling people they have no choice and to "just get on with it." The problem with using this kind of force to blast through resistance is that it erodes people's commitment. They'll comply, but they won't give it their best effort or most creative ideas. That's why the two-step facilitative approach is always superior to the directive telling approach when dealing with resistance. Another important reason for using the two-step approach is that facilitators don't usually have any power over the groups they're working with. When you have no control over people, ordering them to do something they don't want to do usually doesn't work.

Common Conflict Dilemmas

Regardless of how well a session is prepared, there are always things that can go wrong. The following are common facilitation dilemmas and strategies that can help.

Scenario 1: The group resists facilitation. The group desperately needs structure for its discussions, but doesn't like following a step-by-step process. Group members insist they don't want a facilitator. Members say it feels too formal. Sometimes there's a controlling chairperson present and he or she rejects the idea of having a formal facilitator.

Strategy: Offer to facilitate. If rejected, don't hesitate to offer the group methods for tackling the discussion. Facilitate informally: monitor time, ask questions, paraphrase, and synthesize ideas. Make notes and offer summaries.

Potential facilitator mistake: Accepting that the group doesn't want process help and letting it flounder. While it's always best to be able to "officially" facilitate, it's possible to help a group by covertly playing the process role. Some attention to process is better than none.

Scenario 2: Early in the meeting it appears the original agenda is wrong. In spite of data gathering and planning, it becomes clear that the entire premise for the meeting is wrong. The group needs to discuss something else.

Strategy: **Stop the meeting and verify your assessment that the existing agenda is now moot.** Take time to do agenda building. Ask members what they want to achieve at this session. Prioritize the issues and assign times. Take a short break to regroup and create a new process design. Ratify the new agenda with the members. Be flexible and stay focused on the needs of the group.

Potential facilitator mistake: Force the group to follow the original agenda because of the energy and preparation that went into creating the design.

Scenario 3: The meeting goes hopelessly off track Members are usually good at staying focused but have now gone totally off track and refuse to return to the planned agenda.

Strategy: Stop the off-topic discussion and determine whether members are aware that they're off topic and if they're comfortable with this. If they decide they want to stay with this new topic, help them structure their discussion. Ask: *"How long do you want to devote to this? What's the goal of this new discussion? What tools or methods should we use?"* etc.

Facilitate the new discussion. If members decide to return to the original agenda, park the current discussion and return to it at the end of the meeting.

Potential facilitator mistake: Stepping down from the facilitator role because the group isn't following the planned agenda or allowing the group to have a lengthy off-topic discussion without deliberately deciding that this is what members want to do. Trying to force a group back on topic when members feel a pressing need to discuss something else creates unnecessary conflict.

Scenario 4: Group members ignore the process they originally agreed on. There's a clear process for the session, but members ignore it. When you attempt to get people to follow the agreed-upon method, they revert to random discussion.

Strategy: Let them go on this way for a while, then ask: "*How's this going? Are we getting anywhere?*" Once a group has recognized that it isn't making progress, members are often ready to accept a more structured approach.

Potential facilitator mistake: Give up and stop watching for an opening to step back in and offer structure. Take an "I told you so" attitude if members admit frustration.

Scenario 5: The group ignores its own norms. Members have set clear behavioral norms, but start acting in ways that break these rules.

Strategy: Allow them to be dysfunctional for a while, then ask: "*Are the rules that you set being followed? Which rules are being broken and why? What can you do to adhere to these rules?*"

Implement member suggestions. If they don't suggest anything, recommend a few members to be in charge of calling the group's attention to the rules any time they're being broken. Put the onus on members to police themselves.

Potential facilitator mistake: Make verbal interventions without using the power of peer pressure to manage behavior.

Scenario 6: People use the session to unload emotional baggage The agenda is swept off the table as people start venting their frustrations about their jobs, other people, or the organization.

Strategy: Often groups can't focus on the task at hand because of pent-up feelings. In these cases, it's healthy to encourage participants to express their views. The key is to structure this venting so that it can be managed and feelings can be channeled into actions. Useful venting questions include:

> *"How important is it that you share these feelings now?"*

> *"Do we need to have any rules about how we do this?"*

> *"How long should this go on?"*

Potential facilitator mistake: Trying to suppress the venting process or letting it happen without time limits or a plan that leads to action steps.

Scenario 7: No matter what techniques are used, no decision is reached. The group has been discussing options for hours and no clear decision is emerging. Precious time is being wasted.

Strategy: Stop the action and look at the decision method that's being used. There are many decisions that simply can't be made through consensus or voting. Consider using another method like using a decision grid that allows for a more objective rating of individual aspects of competing options.

Another approach is to analyze the blocks to making a final decision by asking the group to identify what's keeping it from making a decision. Record the barriers and spend time removing the key ones.

Potential facilitator mistake: Letting the group spin around for the entire meeting without checking the decision method and/or examining the decision barriers.

Scenario 8: Members refuse to report back their discussions. After a small-group discussion, no one is willing to come forward and present the subgroup's ideas back to the larger group. There's a real concern that one or several of the ideas are too sensitive and that there might be repercussions.

Strategies: Divide the presentation and have two to three members from each group share the spotlight. If there's a lot of material, the whole team can present portions back to the larger group. Also set the stage with the larger group by asking participants to listen with an open mind and not react negatively to the presentation before exploring its potential.

Potential facilitator mistake: Taking the burden from the members and speaking for them. This shifts responsibility for the recommendations from members to yourself, and can result in members taking little responsibility for follow-up actions.

Scenario 9: Members balk at assuming responsibility for action plans. People love discussing problems and brainstorming ideas, but when it comes to action planning, everyone is suddenly too busy or unsure about his or her ability to complete the task.

Strategy: Make it clear that any problem-solving exercise includes action planning and that members will be expected to assume responsibility for implementing their ideas.

Implementing action plans is a growth activity if people are given support and encouragement to go beyond their present capabilities. When people are concerned that they can't succeed, help them identify what materials, training, or other support they need in order to move forward.

If members have time barriers to participating in implementation, these need to be identified and problem-solved. Organizations often ask hardworking people to be on every committee. Considerable thought should be given to whether these individuals have the time to devote to the activity.

Potential facilitator mistake: Letting people off the hook too easily by not problem-solving the blocks or letting a few people shoulder all of the work. The worst strategy of all is to take responsibility for the action steps yourself.

The Facilitative Conflict Management Process

Once the emotions surrounding the situation have been vented, managing conflict collaboratively involves the following eight steps:

1: **Clarify the issue**—Create a clear statement of what the issue is. Ensure that everyone understands that statement.

2: **Make sure appropriate norms are in place**—If things are likely to get emotional, make sure the team has the kind of rules needed to keep people safe and ensure effective behaviors.

3: **Set the time frame for the discussion**—Set limits so that people will know this will not drag on indefinitely.

4: **Explain the process to be used**—The step-by-step approach that will be taken. Emphasize that tools will be used that ensure objectivity and thoroughness.

5: **Analyze the facts of the situation**—Help members gain a shared understanding of the situation. Make sure everyone is heard and that there's a full exploration of all relevant facts.

6: **Generate a range of possible solutions**—Use participative techniques like brainstorming or written brainstorming to create a wide range of potential solutions. Encourage people to build on each other's ideas to further dilute the idea that some ideas are the property of any one person.

7: **Evaluate the solutions**—Establish objective criteria for sorting through all the possible solutions. This can be accomplished by using multi-voting or a form of decision grid.

8: **Plan to implement the highest-ranked solutions**—Ensure that the what, how, who, and when are specified. Troubleshoot the action plan to make sure the steps are doable.

Interpersonal Conflict Worksheet

Helping Behaviors

	Person A	Person B
Leaning forward—listening actively		
Paraphrasing—*"Is this what you're saying?"*		
Questioning to clarify—*"Let me understand this better."*		
Showing respect for the other's opinion—valuing input		
Calmness—voice tone low, relaxed body posture		
Open and vulnerable—showing flexibility		
Clearly stating your position—assertive stance		
Checking for agreement on what is to be resolved		
Laying out ground rules—*"What will help us?"*		
Showing empathy—checking perceptions		
"I" statements—disclosing feelings		
Using other person's name		
Body contact—if appropriate		
Problem solving—looking at alternatives		
Win/win attitude—concern for other person		
Congruence—between verbal and non-verbal behavior		
Feedback—giving specific descriptive details		

Hindering Behaviors

	Person A	Person B
Interrupting/talking too much		
Showing disrespect		
Entrapment questions		
Pushing for solutions		
Arguing about personal perception		
Aggressive manner		
Accusing, laying blame		
Smirking, getting personal		
"You made me" statements		
Non-receptive to suggestions		
Not identifying real feelings		
Incongruity of words and actions		
Defensiveness		
Denying, not owning problems		
Blocking, talking off-topic—changing the subject		
Not giving specific feedback		

Facilitation at a Glance! | Fourth Edition | ©2018 GOAL/QPC

Group Conflict Checklist

Conflict	Comments

No plan or process for approaching the task.
Group wanders from one topic to another because there's no format for discussion. No time is taken at the start of the meeting to establish a process.

Lack of active listening.
Instead of acknowledging each other's points before making their own, people push their own ideas without acknowledging each other.

Personal attacks.
People use a sarcastic tone, ignore each other, interrupt, or even attack each other. They don't focus on the facts.

Lack of process checking.
The group forges ahead without ever stopping to assess whether the process is working or requires modification.

Dominant members.
A few people do all the talking. No one notices or even cares that some people are left out.

Poor time management.
Time isn't budgeted or monitored. Time is wasted on the wrong things.

Folding.
People just give in when things get rough. They don't systematically follow through.

Lack of skill.
There's no evidence that members possess decision-making tools. They also lack basic interpersonal skills.

Passive or nonexistent facilitation.
No one is providing order or policing the action. No notes are kept. Everyone is taking sides. If there's a facilitator, he or she is unwilling to offer procedural options or keep order.

Lack of closure.
The group moves from one topic to another without summarizing or identifying a course of action.

Conflict Effectiveness Survey

Read the following statements and rate how your group currently manages conflict. Be totally honest. Remember that this survey is anonymous. The results will be tabulated and fed back to the group for assessment.

1. Listening

1	2	3	4	5
People assume they're right.			People are open to hearing new ideas.	

2. Acknowledging

1	2	3	4	5
People make points without acknowledging the points made by others.			People acknowledge each other's points even when they don't agree with them.	

3. Objectivity

1	2	3	4	5
We tend to get emotional and argue for our favorite ideas.			We tend to stay calm and look objectively at the facts.	

4. Building

1	2	3	4	5
We tend not to admit that anyone else's ideas are good.			We generally take the ideas of fellow members and try to build on them.	

5. Norms

1	2	3	4	5
We don't have or use norms to manage conflict situations.			We have created a good set of norms that work well to help us manage conflicts.	

6. Trust and Openness

1	2	3	4	5
People don't say what's really on their minds.			There is a lot of trust that you can say whatever you have on your mind.	

7. Approach to Conflict

1	2	3	4	5

Most often we either avoid conflict or argue vehemently.

We tend to collaborate to find solutions we can all live with.

8. Interpersonal Behaviors

1	2	3	4	5

People often become emotional and make personal attacks.

We stay calm and stick to the facts. No one is ever personally attacked.

9. Structure

1	2	3	4	5

We never take a systematic approach. Mostly we just speak our minds.

There is always a clearly defined process for discussions.

10. Closure

1	2	3	4	5

Most of our conflict sessions end without resolution.

We are excellent at getting to solutions and clear action steps.

11. Process Checking

1	2	3	4	5

Once an argument starts we never call time-out and correct ourselves.

We always stop to look at how we're managing our conflicts so we can improve.

12. Time Management

1	2	3	4	5

When things get heated, we lose all track of time and our agenda goes out the window.

We carefully monitor time to make sure we aren't wasting it.

13. Aftermath

1	2	3	4	5

People are usually angry for a long time afterward.

We work at clearing the air of hurt feelings.

FACILITATORS
ENSURE
THAT GROUP
MEMBERS
ENGAGE IN
HEALTHY
DEBATES
INSTEAD OF
DYSFUNCTIONAL
ARGUMENTS.

NINE

MEETING MANAGEMENT

One of the key facilitator roles is to know how to design and manage effective meetings. Features of many **ineffective** meetings include:

Direction

❏ lack of clarity about the meeting goal

❏ a vague or nonexistent agenda

❏ no time limits on discussions

❏ no discernible process for working on important issues

❏ no one facilitating discussions

❏ people haven't done their homework

❏ discussions that go off track or spin in circles

❏ lack of closure to discussions before moving on

❏ arguing points of view rather than debating ideas

❏ a few people dominating while others sit passively

❏ ending without detailed action plans for next steps

❏ absence of process checking during the meeting

❏ no evaluation at the end.

Meetings that Work

Here are the ingredients shared by all **effective** meetings:

❑ a detailed agenda that spells out what the goals of
the discussion will be, who is bringing each item
forward, and an estimate of how long each item
will take

❑ clear process notes that describe the tools and
techniques that will be used

❑ assigned roles such as facilitator, chairperson,
minute taker, and timekeeper

❑ a set of group norms created by the members and
posted in the meeting room

❑ clarity about decision-making options to be used

❑ effective member behaviors

❑ periodic process checks

❑ clear conflict-management strategies

❑ a process that creates true closure

❑ detailed and clear minutes

❑ specific follow-up plans

❑ a post-meeting evaluation.

Our Meetings Are Terrible!

On the next page are some of the symptoms of dysfunctional meetings and prescriptions for their cure. These
are, of course, easier to identify than to fix, but if you can
help team members become
aware of their patterns, they
can begin to resolve them.

dysfunctional

Meeting Behaviors - Symptoms and Cures

Symptoms	Cures
As one person finishes speaking, the next starts a new topic. There's no building on ideas or continuity.	Each person acknowledges the comments of the last speaker. Finish a point before moving on.
People argue their views, rather than understanding the issue or anyone else's input. Lack of listening.	Train members to paraphrase what is said in response to their point. Use chart to record/view all sides.
A problem is mentioned and someone announces that he or she understands it. A solution is proposed and discussion moves on.	Use a systematic approach to bring structure to discussions. Become thorough in solving problems. Avoid jumping to solutions.
Whenever someone disagrees with a group decision, the dissenting view is ignored.	Develop an ear for dissenting views and make sure they are heard. Have someone else paraphrase the dissenting opinion.
The group uses brainstorming and voting to make most decisions.	Pre-plan meeting processes so other tools are on hand, and then use them.
Conversations often go nowhere. In frustration, the group moves on to a new topic without closure.	Set time limits on discussions and periodically evaluate them. Use summaries to achieve closure.
People often speak in an emotional tone of voice. Sometimes they even say things that are personal.	Have people stop and rephrase their comments so there are no distracting personal innuendoes.
People use side-chats to share their thoughts.	Encourage honesty by valuing all input. Draw side-chatterers back to group conversation.
Group members don't notice they've become sidetracked on an issue until they've been off topic for quite a while.	Call "time-out" or have some other signal to flag off-track conversations. Decide whether you want to digress or park the particular issue.
The extroverts, or powerful, do most of the talking. Some people say little at most meetings.	Use round robins to obtain input. Call members by name. Use idea slips to get written comments.
No one notices body language; people are agitated or tuned out.	Make perception checks and ask people to express their feelings.
There is no closure to most topics. Little action takes place between meetings.	Stress closure. Reach a clear decision and record it. Use an action planning form for next meeting.
There is no after-meeting evaluation. People debrief in their offices.	Do a meeting evaluation and discuss the results before the next meeting. Post new rules or improvement ideas.

The Fundamentals of Meeting Management

1. Create and Use a Detailed Agenda

Develop agenda ahead of time and have the team ratify it. Advance agendas allow members to do homework and come prepared to make decisions. Agendas include:

❏ name of each topic, its purpose, and its expected outcome

❏ time guidelines for each agenda item

❏ the name of the person bringing each item forward

❏ the details of the process to be used for each discussion.

If the agenda can't be designed in advance, it should be the first order of business. In this facilitated discussion, members design the agenda for that day's session.

 A clear agenda circulated in advance is key to success.

2. Develop Step-by-Step Process Notes

Most of the books about meetings do not mention *Process Notes*, largely because these books are geared toward meetings that will be chaired rather than facilitated. These detailed process notes specify how the discussion will be facilitated. They specify the tools to be used and how participation will be managed.

In the following sample agenda, we've added process notes to illustrate their important role. It's often a good idea to openly share the process notes with the group.

Sample Agenda with Process Notes

Name of group:	**Customer Fulfillment Team**
Members:	**Jane, Muhammad, Jacques, Elaine, Carl, Fred, Diane, Joe**
Meeting details:	**Monday, June 12, 11:00 – 1:00 (Brown Bag Lunch), Conference Room C**

Meeting Process Notes

What & Why	How (process notes)
Warm-up (10 min) ○ Joe; create focus	Members each share one recent customer contact story.
Review agenda and norms (5 min) ○ Joe; set context	Ratify the agenda and the norms through general discussion. Add new items; make sure there is clarity about the overall goal of the meeting.
Bring forward action items (25 min) ○ all members; implementation-monitoring	Brief report-back by all members on action plans created at the last meeting; addition of any new plans.
Focus group updates (20 min) ○ Jacques & Diane; identify areas for improvement	Report on the outcomes of six customer focus groups. Use force-field analysis to distinguish between what we are doing well and what we aren't.
Prioritization of customer issues (20 min) ○ Joe; set priorities	Establish criteria to evaluate customer concerns. Use criteria matrix to appraise each issue and identify priorities for action.
Problem solving of priority issues (30 min) ○ entire group; create improvement plans	Divide into two sub-teams to problem solve the two top-priority issues; create detailed action plans for the top issues; meet as a group to share and ratify ideas.
Next-step planning and agenda building (10 min) ○ Joe; ensure closure and design next session	Make sure people know what they're expected to work on; create agenda for next meeting.
Exit survey (10 min) ○ Joe; check meeting effectiveness	Have people evaluate the meeting on their way out the door. Identify items to be brought forward at the next meeting.

3. Clarify Roles and Responsibilities

Effective meetings require people to play defined roles.

Chairperson: Runs the meeting according to defined rules, but also offers opinions and engages in the discussion if he or she chooses. The chairperson has traditionally not been neutral. Most often, the chairperson of any meeting is the official leader, who plays an active role as both decision maker and opinion leader.

Facilitator: Designs the methodology for the meeting, manages participation, offers useful tools, helps the group determine its needs, keeps things on track, and periodically checks on how things are going. A facilitator doesn't influence what, but instead focuses on how, the meeting topic is being discussed. A facilitator is a procedural expert who is there to help and support the group's effectiveness.

 Clarifying roles helps reduce power struggles.

Minute taker: Takes brief, accurate notes of what's discussed and the decisions made. Also responsible for incorporating any notes on flip charts. Most often, minute-taking responsibilities are rotated among the regular members of a work group. However, for special meetings or if resources allow, this role can be assigned to a neutral outsider.

Timekeeper: A rotating role in which someone keeps track of the time and reminds the group about milestones periodically. This role is not a license to be autocratic or to shut down important discussions if they're running over. The use of an automatic timer will allow the timekeeper to participate in the discussion.

Scribe: A group member who volunteers to help the facilitator by recording group comments on a flip chart. This has the benefit of freeing the facilitator from the distraction of writing, but adds its own complications. The scribe may start facilitating or may not take accurate notes.

Since having a scribe takes an additional person out of the discussion, it is an impractical strategy for small groups. Facilitators make their own notes and, if a scribe is used, clarifying questions should go through the facilitator.

Balancing the Roles of Chairperson and Facilitator

Chairing and facilitating are two distinct meeting management roles. Chairing is most useful at the start of a meeting in order to review past minutes, share information, and manage a round-robin report-back by members. Chairing traditionally relies on the use of pre-published rules of order.

Since chairs are not neutral, their major drawback is that they tend to influence decisions and concentrate power. It's not uncommon for a strong chairperson to make final decisions on important items.

A consequence of this decision mode is that the chair owns the outcome. There's also little emphasis on using process tools by traditional chairpersons.

Facilitating is designed to foster the full and equal participation of all members for items on which their input is needed. Because facilitators are neutral, they empower members. They rely on consensus and collaboration so the whole group feels it has ownership.

A common role arrangement is a leader who uses a chairperson approach to start the meeting and review the agenda, take care of the housekeeping and information-sharing portions, and then switch to facilitation to obtain feedback.

Know when and how to act as an effective chairperson. Conversely, it would be ideal if all chairpersons were also skilled facilitators who could switch roles whenever it was desirable to get participation and ownership.

With advance planning, these roles don't need to conflict. The key is to remember that each has its place and to be clear about which approach is used in which situations.

Balancing Meeting Roles

Chair when you want to:	Facilitate when you want to:
Review past minutes & agenda items	Get participation and shift ownership
Hear members report back or exchange information	Engage people in planning, problem solving, or relationship building
Remain accountable for decisions	Get members to make decisions

4. Set Clear Meeting Norms

Define clear norms for behavior that are created by the group. Help the group tailor its norms to meet the demands of particular meetings by engaging members in setting targeted norms if they are needed.

5. Manage Participation

Include everyone in the discussion. Ensure that structure exists for each item, that there's effective use of decision-making tools, and that closure is achieved for all items. Facilitators are responsible for ensuring that members know and exhibit effective group behaviors. If members lack group skills, facilitators can conduct simple training exercises.

6. Make Periodic Process Checks

Process checking is used during meetings to keep things on track. This involves stopping the discussion periodically to redirect member attention to how the meeting is going. The purpose of this shift in focus is to engage members in a quick review in order to identify needed improvements.

The ABCs of process checking:

A. **Check the purpose**: Ask members whether they're still clear about the focus of the meeting, to make sure everyone is still on the same page.

   WHEN: If the conversation seems to be stuck or if people seem to be confused; at least once per session.

B. **Check the process**: Ask if the tool or approach being used is working or needs changing. Is progress being made? Ask for or offer approach suggestions.

   WHEN: The process tool being used isn't yielding results, or it's evident that the process isn't being followed as originally designed.

C. **Check the pace**: When things seem to be dragging or moving too fast; any time there are signs that people look frustrated; or are losing focus.

   WHEN: Any time people seem restless, at least every twenty minutes, at a minimum, at least once per session.

D. **Check the people**: Ask members how they're feeling: Are they energized? Tired? Satisfied, Frustrated? Ask for suggestions on how to change energy levels.

   WHEN: Any time people look distracted, frustrated, or tired; at least once during each session.

One of the most common challenges in meetings is when the wheels start spinning and the discussion gets stuck. Conduct and intervene with a process check:

   "I'm noticing that points are repeated but nothing is being decided."

   "Are you stuck? Why is this happening?"

   "Is anyone confused about the topic under discussion?"

   "Is the approach working or do we need to try something else?"

   "Are we moving too fast, too slow?"

   "How are people feeling? What can we do to start moving again?"

Although process checks are usually done verbally, they can also be conducted in the form of a survey posted on a flip chart. Members are invited to anonymously rate how the meeting is going, usually as they leave the room for a break. When members return, they interpret the survey results and brainstorm ideas for improving the remainder of the session. All practical suggestions are implemented.

Meeting Process Check Survey

Purpose: To what extent are you clear about our goals?

1	2	3	4	5
Poor	Fair	Satisfactory	Good	Excellent

Progress: To what extent are we achieving our goals?

1	2	3	4	5
Poor	Fair	Satisfactory	Good	Excellent

Pace: How does the pace feel?

1	2	3	4	5
Far too slow	Slow	Just right	Fast	Far too fast

Pulse: How are you feeling about the session?

1	2	3	4	5
Frustrated	Exhausted	Satisfied	Pleased	Energized

7. Determine Next Steps

Never let a group leave a meeting without clear next steps in place. Define tasks, including by whom and when they will be completed. These actions need to be brought forward at all subsequent meetings to make sure that the group is following up on commitments.

8. Evaluate the Meeting

Effective groups make a habit of routinely evaluating meeting effectiveness. Three basic ways to evaluate a meeting:

1. Conduct a Force-Field Analysis – This involves asking:

    "What were the strengths of today's meeting?" **(+)**

    "What were the weaknesses?" **(–)**

    "What's the prescription to correct each weakness?" **(Rx)**

2. Post an Exit Survey—Three or four questions are written on flip chart paper and posted near an exit. Members answer the questions on the chart paper upon leaving the meeting. The results are brought forward and discussed at the start of the next meeting.

3. Implement a Written Survey—Create a survey and distribute it to members to complete anonymously. After tabulation, the results are discussed at a subsequent meeting. This is an appropriate exercise to be done three or four times a year for any ongoing group or team.

> Meetings need to end with true closure.

Meeting Exit Survey

Output: To what extent did we achieve what we needed to?

1	2	3	4	5
Poor	Fair	Satisfactory	Good	Excellent

Organization: How effective was the meeting structure?

1	2	3	4	5
Poor	Fair	Satisfactory	Good	Excellent

Use of time: How well did we use our time?

1	2	3	4	5
Poor	Fair	Satisfactory	Good	Excellent

Participation: How did we do on making sure everyone was involved equally?

1	2	3	4	5
Poor	Fair	Satisfactory	Good	Excellent

Decision Making: How well thought out were our decisions?

1	2	3	4	5
Poor	Fair	Satisfactory	Good	Excellent

Action Plans: How clear and doable are our action plans?

1	2	3	4	5
Poor	Fair	Satisfactory	Good	Excellent

Limit exit surveys to three or four questions. Implement the next survey to create impetus for improving meetings.

Meeting Effectiveness Survey

To be completed anonymously to the facilitator for review.

1. PREPARATION
Does everyone come prepared and ready to make decisions?

1	2	3	4	5
We are often unprepared			We are always well prepared	

2. COMMUNICATION
Are agendas circulated to all members in advance of the meeting?

1	2	3	4	5
Agendas are rarely circulated in advance		Are always circulated in advance		

3. SETTING
Is there a quiet place with ample space and support materials?

1	2	3	4	5
The meeting place is not well suited			The meeting place is excellent	

4. MEETING OBJECTIVES
Are objectives and expected outcomes clearly set for agenda items?

1	2	3	4	5
Objective/outcomes are never clear		Objectives/outcomes are always clear		

5. START TIMES/END TIMES
Do meetings start/end on time?

1	2	3	4	5
Meetings hardly ever start/end on time			Meetings always start/end on time	

6. ROLE CLARITY
Are roles such as timekeeper, scribe, and facilitator clearly defined?

1	2	3	4	5
Roles are not always clearly defined			Roles clearly defined	

7. PAST MEETING REVIEW
Are action items from the previous meeting(s) brought forward?

1	2	3	4	5
Previous items are seldom brought forward		Previous items are brought forward		

8. PROCESS/MINUTES KEPT
Is there clarity before each topic as to how it will be managed?

1	2	3	4	5
There is rarely any structured process		There is always a structured process		

9. INTERRUPTIONS/PACE
Are meetings being disrupted due to people leaving, texting, web surfing, etc.?

1	2	3	4	5

There are constant interruptions · We control interruptions

10. PARTICIPATION/LISTENING
Are members fully engaged and listening?

1	2	3	4	5

People hold back · Everyone takes part

11. CONFLICT MANAGEMENT
Are differences of opinion suppressed, or is conflict effectively used?

1	2	3	4	5

We tend to argue emotionally · We debate objectively

12. DECISION-MAKING QUALITY
Does the group generally make high-quality decisions?

1	2	3	4	5

We tend to make low-quality decisions · We make high-quality decisions

13. LEADERSHIP
Is there a shared or singular use of authority?

1	2	3	4	5

A few people make most decisions · Decision making is shared

14. TRACKING
Do meetings stay on track and follow the agenda?

1	2	3	4	5

Meetings usually stray off track · Meetings usually stay on track

16. CLOSURE
Do we effectively end topics before moving on to new ones?

1	2	3	4	5

We move on without closure · We close each topic before moving on

17. FOLLOW-UP
Is there timely, effective follow-up to commitments made during the meetings?

1	2	3	4	5

We tend not to follow up · There is consistent follow-up

THE ALL-IMPORTANT STATUS UPDATE MEETINGS

The type of meeting that takes place most often in both projects and in department is the *Status Update Meeting*. These meetings happen anywhere from once a month to several times a week.

Status Update Meetings are about exchanging information: they are just for information sharing and updates. This includes presentations and reports about the status of any work in progress.

Status Update Meetings are designed purely to make sure that everyone is in the loop. They're not designed to generate a lot of discussion. That's what helps keep them short and crisp.

This parameter needs to be stated explicitly at the beginning of each *Status Update Meeting* so that everyone is clear about the scope. Issues or differing points of view should be noted and taken off-line for further discussion at a well-structured decision-making meeting.

It's important to note that there is actually very little facilitation in these types of meetings. Since there is very little group decision making, the role of the leader is to act like the chairperson who ensures that everyone gets a chance to report and to keep the meeting moving along.

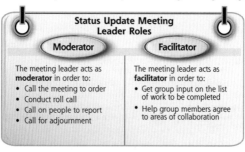

Status Update Meeting Leader Roles

Moderator	Facilitator
The meeting leader acts as **moderator** in order to: • Call the meeting to order • Conduct roll call • Call on people to report • Call for adjournment	The meeting leader acts as **facilitator** in order to: • Get group input on the list of work to be completed • Help group members agree to areas of collaboration

The Status-Update Meeting Format*

While *Status Update Meeting* formats vary, most include the following standard items:

Roll call. Invite meeting participants to share their names, the areas they represent and their role in the project.

Accomplishments. Ask everyone, in turn, to list their most recent developments and successes. Record these in the minutes.

The status of work. Go around the group to hear updates on progress as compared to what was originally planned, unexpected wins, or issues that others should be aware of.

Work scheduled but not complete. Review any items on the work plan that were scheduled to be completed but have not been started or are behind schedule. Explore the reasons for any delays and commit to new target dates.

Project Issues. Identify any ongoing issues affecting the project that could impact progress and have not been resolved. Identify who needs to work on which specific problems.

Imminent actions. Ask each team member to offer a quick snapshot of what they're doing next and anything they need from other members of the team to support their action.

*Adapted from The Project Meeting Facilitator by Tammy Adams and Jan Means.

Facilitating Virtual Meetings

There is a growing trend toward online meetings. Virtual meetings are less interacting and more disconnected. Special challenges of virtual meetings include:

- if video isn't present the meetings tend to feel impersonal and disconnected

- if people can't see each other interaction tends to be stilted and conversations tend toward one-way information sharing

- since people have to wait for a chance to talk, meetings can drag on far too long

- sometimes people sit in silence for long stretches listening to conversations that don't involve them

- if there isn't video, it's impossible to read body language to pick up on the nonverbal clues that identify how people are engaged or are feeling

- if differences of opinion crop up, it's very difficult to manage the conflict effectively, bring other people into the conversation, or help the parties arrive at a mutually agreeable solution

- while minutes are usually sent out afterward, there are no flip-chart notes being taken during conversations to keep everyone focused and to help the conversation flow

- participants often do other tasks during the session like reading, eating, and email rather than paying attention

- it's easy for people to walk in and out of a virtual phone meeting without detection by the other participants.

Design virtual meetings to include only those things that need real-time interaction. Send PDF packets for review beforehand. Detail what needs to be done before the session and what will be handled during the session. Use calls/video to become acquainted, discuss problems, jointly search for solutions, make decisions, ratify action plans, clarify work assignments, etc.

Facilitation at a Glance! | Fourth Edition | ©2018 GOAL/QPC

As with any face-to-face meeting, a virtual meeting needs an agenda that is circulated ahead of time and that specifically describes the objectives and expected outcomes of the meeting.

Provide a clear purpose, describe the process, conduct a warm-up exercise, make interventions, call on people by name, conduct periodic process checks, paraphrase key ideas, offer periodic summaries, ensure that key items have closure, and provide clear action steps.

Before the Virtual Meeting:

- Contact participants by phone or e-mail to seek their input on the agenda
- Create a detailed agenda, with process notes, that identifies the various types of conversations that will be held (information sharing, planning, problem solving, relationship building)
- Identify who needs to be involved and for which segments of the call, plus the information that each player needs to prepare
- Distribute the agenda to participants so they can do their homework and call/be online at the proper time.

At the Start of the Virtual Meeting:

- Conduct a roll call to establish that people are engaged and ready to proceed. If applicable, invite each person to state what he or she wants to get out of the meeting. Record these personal goals and refer to them throughout the meeting to help keep people engaged and let them know you have them in mind
- Create a name map on a blank sheet of paper in front of you. Beside each name, write down the person's stated goal for the session. As the meeting progresses, make a check mark beside people's names every time they speak. This will remind you of who is on the line and what each of them needs from the session. It will

also help you identify the people who need to be brought into the conversation

o Review the agenda to clarify the overall purpose of the call, the purpose and process for individual segments, and the time associated with each segment. Also be clear about who needs to be part of which conversations

o Clarify the rules of the meeting. This can be a facilitated conversation, or you can propose a core set of rules that participants can amend and ratify.

 Virtual meetings require their own targeted norms.

Norms for Virtual Meetings

To ensure that this call is productive, we will all:

o be as clear and concise as possible

o engage others with questions and offer your opinion

o ask for clarification if it's needed

o freely express concerns and opinions

o speak up if we notice we've been silent for too long or if a particular conversation needs to wrap up

o strive to stay focused; avoid doing other tasks

o ask for a summary any time we need to refocus

o announce when we are leaving the call.

During the Virtual Meeting

o At the start of each topic, review the purpose, process, and time frame for each item.

o Direct by name, both to present and to comment on what's been said. Keep track of who is getting airtime.

o Periodically make process checks to ensure that things are still on track.

The Virtual Meeting Process Check:

> Is the purpose still clear?
>
> Is our approach working? Are we making progress?
>
> Is the pace okay? . . . too fast? . . . too slow?
>
> Have we lost anyone?

- To bring closure to a topic, offer a summary of the key points that were made. If it was a decision-making discussion, turn the summary into a decision statement, then conduct a roll call to ask meeting participants to accept the final decision
- Help the group create action plans for any topics that need them. Encourage people to take responsibility for follow-through.

At the End of the Virtual Meeting:

- Review the summaries for each topic and the action steps that have been identified
- Invite each person to say whether his or her goal for the meeting has been achieved or to make a statement of what he or she takes from the meeting
- Conduct a brief post-meeting evaluation by asking people to identify what worked or did not work and to offer ideas to improve future sessions. If this is impractical, create an evaluation form online and deploy it through e-mail
- Share details about when and how the minutes will be shared
- Identify any future teleconferences
- Express thanks for everyone's participation and sign off.

Meeting Best Practices
Part One

Pre-meeting:

o Use emails and mechanisms like surveys as an alternative to meetings wherever possible to reduce the amount of face-to-face time needed.

o Identify who needs to attend which portions of the meeting and invite only those who are essential.

o Circulate a detailed agenda that describes the objectives and the times for each topic so that participants can prepare.

To Start:

o Begin with a review of the topics and the expected outcomes for each.

o Reiterate the meeting guidelines and ask if any additional rules are needed for that meeting.

o Ask someone to help you manage the time, or set up an automatic timer.

o Set up a Parking Lot sheet of paper and explain that you will use it to capture all topics that are best addressed at another time.

o Before starting each new topic, identify the nature of the discussion. Is it to share information, plan strategy, solve a problem or build relationships?

o Start each discussion by clarifying the purpose of the conversation, the expected outcomes, the process to be used and the timeframe.

o For each new agenda item, also clarify whether the group members are empowered to make the decision or are simply being asked for their input for a decision that will be made elsewhere.

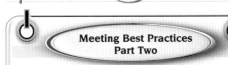

During Discussions:

o Monitor time and mention time milestones tactfully.

o Point out any off-topic items and ask permission to place them into the *Parking Lot*.

o Keep track of speakers and call on quiet people.

o Regardless of whether or not you're neutral during a specific discussion, make accurate notes on a flip chart to capture member's ideas.

o Ping-pong ideas around to ensure that there's conversation between group members.

o Conduct periodic process checks. Ask people if they feel progress is being made, if the process seems to be working, if the pace seems right, and how people are feeling.

o Summarize periodically, especially during complicated discussions, to make sure that key ideas are being fully understood and to refocus attention.

To Wrap Up:

o Start to wrap up ten minutes before the scheduled end of the meeting.

o Give clear summaries of all the main points shared at the meeting, especially the decisions that were made.

o Review all action plans. Include a description of what completion looks like, responsibilities and due dates.

o Schedule the next meeting.

o Invite people to provide feedback as they exit.

FACILITATORS
PROVIDE TOOLS
TO BRING
MUCH NEEDED
STRUCTURE
TO COMPLEX
DECISION-MAKING
CONVERSATIONS.

Chapter TEN

PROCESS TOOLS FOR FACILITATORS

Since scores of process tools exist, it would be impossible to explain them all. This chapter represents the basic processes that every facilitator should know how and when to use:

Appreciative Review	The 5 Whys
S.W.O.T.	Decision Grid
S.O.A.R.	Troubleshooting
Visioning	Exit Survey
Brainstorming	Survey Feedback
Force-Field Analysis	Needs and Offers Dialogue
Gap Analysis	Gallery Walk
Multi-Voting	Systematic Problem Solving
Root-Cause Analysis	

In addition to these tools, all facilitators should learn the techniques associated with quality improvement such as process mapping, affinity diagrams, storyboarding, histograms, scatter diagrams, and critical path charts. *The Memory Jogger*® 2, from GOAL/QPC is an excellent resource for all these quality improvement tools.

Appreciative Review

What is it? A positive discussion about the past in which group members answer questions about recent events to explore all of the good things that have happened.

When should you use it? When the morale of a group has sagged. Very useful during the mid-point check meeting of any project. When it supports the effectiveness of the team to remember all of the positive things that they have accomplished and to appreciate each other. Great at the start of a strategic-planning meeting before looking forward. Should be part of any discussion to help restart a team that has fizzled out.

What does it do? It encourages group members to reflect on all that they have accomplished and all of the positive things that they have going for them. Also gives individual group members a feeling that they have contributed and are valued by others.

What's the outcome? Group members have an opportunity to reflect on the good things that have taken place. They also receive public recognition for their contribution. This lifts the spirits of the members and reenergizes them for the work ahead.

Steps to Do an Appreciative Review

1: Create a series of questions similar to the ones below:

   a Looking back over the last few months, what have we accomplished?

   b. What has been our greatest achievement? What makes us most proud?

   c. What outside factors helped us achieve those successes?

   d What role did each of us play to achieve that?

   e. What lessons did we learn during our recent work?

   f. What excites us about the opportunities ahead?

2 : If the group has fewer than six members, facilitate a discussion of all of the questions in the total group. If the group is larger, break the group into subgroups of three or four members. Ask these subgroups to answer the first three questions and make notes so they can share their answers with the larger group.

3 : Bring the members back together and ask each subgroup to share what they discussed while you record answers on a flip chart or electronic board.

4 : Pose the question about what each person contributed to the whole group. Allow a minute or two for quiet reflection. Invite each person to speak about their contribution to the success of the group. If someone is downplaying his or her role, invite others to point out what they've seen that person contribute. It's not necessary to record this conversation. What matters is that it takes place publicly.

5 : Ask group members to form new subgroups so that they get to talk to others in the group. Pose the remaining two questions. Ask someone in each sub group to take notes.

6 : Bring the members back together again to share their answers to the last two questions. Record all comments at the front of the room.

S.W.O.T.

What is it? A fundamental analysis tool useful at the start of strategic conversations. The letters stand for **Strengths, Weaknesses, Opportunities, and Threats.**

When should you use it? To provide a framework at the start of a strategic-planning activity. To gather data about the environment.

What's its purpose? To create a balanced picture of both the positives and negatives that need to be taken into consideration during the planning process.

What's the outcome? S.W.O.T. fosters a constructive, growth-oriented, and possibility-focused understanding of the organization's potential.

Steps to Do a S.W.O.T. Analysis

1 : Circulate the questions associated with the four categories of inquiry to allow time to reflect and prepare.

2 : For a group of fewer than twelve individuals, facilitate a group discussion in which the questions are explored and discussed in depth. Record key ideas. In a large group, create small groups of three or four people. Allow fifteen to twenty minutes for discussion of the questions in all four categories.

3 : Create areas around the room where people can gather in small groups to share and record their ideas. Use the steps described in this chapter for the Gallery Walk process to encourage dialogue and to gather ideas.

A Sample S.W.O.T. Analysis:
Strengths
  ○ What are we doing really well?
  ○ What are our greatest assets?
  ○ What are we most proud of accomplishing?
  ○ What makes us unique?

- o What do our strengths tell us about our skills?
- o How do we use our strengths to get results?

Weaknesses

- o What aren't we doing well?
- o What are our greatest liabilities?
- o In what areas have we underperformed?
- o What are our limitations in resources, staff, technology?
- o What do our weaknesses tell us about ourselves?
- o What are some of the reasons that we have not yet overcome our weaknesses?

Opportunities

- o What are the most profound changes shaping our environment?
- o What innovation inspires us to change?
- o How can we make a difference for the organization and its stakeholders?
- o What are the top three opportunities we should focus our efforts on?
- o How can we reframe weaknesses or threats so they become opportunities?
- o What are our customers asking us to do?
- o What synergies can we create with other groups?

Threats

- o Who or what is our biggest competitor or danger?
- o What is the competition doing that could harm us?
- o What would be the worst thing that we could do?
- o What threat have we underestimated or failed to consider?
- o What threats do our weaknesses expose us to?

S.O.A.R.

What is it? A strength-based analysis tool useful at the start of strategic conversations. It is a more positive version of the well-known S.W.O.T. Analysis. The letters stand for **Strengths, Opportunities, Aspirations, and Results.**

When should you use it? To set a positive tone for planning conversations. At the start of strategic retreats. To reframe the current situation in positive terms in situations where issues of low morale need to be addressed.

What's its purpose? To create an upward spiral of thought, action, and behavior. To encourage creativity and out-of-the-box thinking. To guide strategic thinking toward the possible, without being hampered by the negatives.

What's the outcome? S.O.A.R. fosters a constructive, growth-oriented, and possibility-focused understanding of the organization's potential.

Steps to Do a S.O.A.R. Analysis

1 : Circulate the questions associated with the four categories of inquiry to allow participants time to prepare.

2 : For groups of fewer than twelve, facilitate a group discussion in which the questions are explored and discussed in depth. Record key ideas. In a large group, create small groups of three or four people. Allow fifteen to twenty minutes for discussion of the questions in all four categories.

3 : Create areas around the room where people can gather in small groups to share and record their ideas. Use the steps described in this chapter for the Gallery Walk process to encourage dialogue and to gather ideas.

A S.O.A.R. Sample:

Strengths

  o What are we doing really well?

  o What are our greatest assets?

  o What are we most proud of accomplishing?

  o What makes us unique?

  o What do our strengths tell us about our skills?

  o How do we use our strengths to get results?

Opportunities

  o How do we collectively understand outside threats?

  o Top three opportunities we should focus our efforts on?

  o What is the organization asking us to do?

  o How can we best partner with our customers?

  o What synergies can we create with other groups?

Aspirations

  o When we explore our values and aspirations, what are we deeply passionate about?

  o What's our most compelling aspiration? Who should we become?

  o How do we allow our values to drive our vision?

  o How can we make a difference for all stakeholders?

Results

  o With our strengths, opportunities, and aspirations, what would indicate we're on track for achieving our goals?

  o What do we want to be known for?

  o How do we tangibly translate our strengths, opportunities, and aspirations?

Visioning

What is it? A highly participative approach to goal setting.

When should you use it? When members need to clarify their own thoughts and then share those ideas with each other to create a shared statement of the desired future.

What's its purpose? Allows people to put forward their ideas. Makes sure everyone is involved and heard from. Creates energy. Helps people to align. Gives people an interactive method to identify a group goal.

What's the outcome? The visioning process is very participative and energizes everyone in the room. It also creates buy-in because the group's direction is coming from the members themselves. Everyone is involved at once. All ideas are heard. This is a great way to conduct goal-setting with a group.

Steps to Do Visioning

1 : Post a series of questions that relate to the task and ask how the final outcome ought to look at a future point in time. The vision questions will always be different, of course, depending on the situation.

Sample Visioning Questions for a Customer Service Improvement Team:

Imagine that it's exactly two years from today:

  "Describe how you now serve customers."

  "What specific improvements have been made?"

"What are people saying about the team now?"

"What problems has the group solved?"

"What specific outcomes have been achieved?"

"How are people behaving differently?"

2: Ask each person to write down his or her own responses to the questions. Allow at least five minutes. Give more time if needed. Ask people not to speak to each other during this writing phase.

3: Ask everyone to find a partner. Ideally, this is the person he or she knows least. Allocate three to five minutes for the first partner to share his or her vision. Ask the other partner to facilitate. After three to five minutes, ask the partners to switch roles so that the second person can talk.

4: When time is up, ask everyone to find a second partner. Repeat the process outlined in Step #3, only allow slightly less time per person. Encourage people to steal any good ideas they heard from their last partners and incorporate these into their own visions.

5: Repeat the process again with new partners. This time, limit the exchange to one to three minutes per person in order to encourage people to prioritize and share key points. You can stop after only a few rounds or continue until everyone has spoken to everyone else.

6: Ask people to return to their original seats. Begin facilitating a discussion to pull the ideas together. You'll find that ideas have become fairly homogenized by this point.

Brainstorming

What is it? A synergistic technique that frees people to think creatively and generate innovative ideas.

When should you use it? When it's advantageous to generate a free flow of creative ideas that are not bound by the usual barriers. To involve everyone. To create energy. To generate a wide range of potential ideas.

What's its purpose? Allows exploration of new ideas and challenges traditional thinking. Lets people share ideas without fear of being corrected or challenged. It separates the creation of ideas from the evaluation activity.

What's the outcome? A wide range of creative ideas. Because brainstorming frees people from practical considerations, it encourages them to think creatively. It's also an energizing process that helps move people to take action. Because it's highly participative, brainstorming makes everyone feel they're an important part of the solution.

Steps to Do Brainstorming

1 : Announce that you will be using brainstorming. Review the rules:

- o Let ideas flow
- o There are no bad ideas
- o Be creative
- o Think in new ways
- o Build on others' ideas
- o Break out of old patterns
- o Keep discussion moving
- o No evaluation until later.

2 : Clarify the topic being brainstormed, then allow some quiet-time for people to think about solutions.

3: Ask members to let their ideas flow. While you can brainstorm by going round robin around the group, brainstorming is best done spontaneously with members offering ideas as they come to mind.

4: Record ideas as they're generated. Do not discuss or elaborate on them. Keep it moving.

5: When people have run out of ideas, generate additional ideas by asking probing questions such as:

"What if money were no object?"

"What would our competitors wish we would do?"

"What's the opposite of something already suggested?"

6: When the flow of ideas has stopped, explore each brainstormed idea in detail so that it's fully developed and clearly understood. Combine like ideas that are simply worded differently.

7: Use a decision grid, affinity diagram, or multi-voting to sort the ideas.

Written Brainstorming

What is it? A private and individual idea-generation technique in which people write down their ideas, then pass them to other group members who build on them.

When should you use it? When people are reluctant to speak in front of others, or when there are outspoken members who might dominate a traditional brainstorming session. Also useful if the issue or topic is sensitive, since the initial idea-generation step is anonymous and private.

What's its purpose? The anonymity of this tool encourages people to express their ideas.

What's the outcome? A lot of ideas are generated in a short time. It also allows people to learn others' ideas in an anonymous setting.

Steps to Do Written Brainstorming

anonymous related ideas

1 : Clarify the topic or issue for which ideas will be generated. Explain the process to members.

2 : Give each person small slips of sticky paper. Ask members to work alone to think of ideas that relate to the topic being discussed. Allow anywhere from three to ten minutes for the idea-generation step.

3 : Ask members to fold their anonymous idea slips and toss them onto the center of the table.

4 : Mix the slips and ask each person to take back as many as he or she tossed in. If anyone pulls out his or her own slip, that person can toss it back or exchange it with a neighbor.

5 : Each person now has three to five minutes to think of additional ideas based on the thoughts stimulated by reading the ideas picked from the pile. These new slips should be thrown into the middle of the table and then tossed and also distributed.

6 : Once all ideas have been distributed, ask members to read aloud all the ideas on the slips they drew from the pile.

7 : Discuss each idea so that it is fully understood. Do not try to find out who suggested each idea. Stick all the slips on a wall or on flip charts.

8 : Use a decision grid or multi-voting to sort the most effective ideas to fit the situation.

Force-Field Analysis

What is it? Force-field analysis is a structured method of looking at the two opposing forces acting on a situation.

When should you use it? When you need to surface all of the factors at play in a situation so that barriers and problems can be identified. It also encourages members to make a balanced assessment of a situation.

What's its purpose? Clarifies the resources available and also the barriers or obstacles. Helps the group to gain an understanding of the forces acting on its work.

What's the outcome? Force-field analysis is a valuable tool for analyzing situations and identifying problems that need to be solved. It helps groups make more effective decisions because it lets members look at both positive and negative forces at play.

Steps to Do Force-Field Analysis

1 : Identify a topic, situation, or project; for example: computer training.

2 : Help the group state the goal of the discussion: "All staff to receive training in the new operating system in three weeks."

3 : Draw a line down the center of a flip-chart sheet. Use one side to identify all of the forces (resources, skills, attitudes) that will help reach the goal. On the other side, identify all the forces that could hinder reaching the goal (barriers, problems, deficiencies, etc.).

4: Once all the help and hinder elements have been identified, use multi-voting or a decision matrix to determine which of the hindrances or barriers are a priority for immediate problem solving.

5: Address the priority barriers using the Systematic Problem-Solving Model.

Variations of Force-Field Analysis

Force-field analysis has many variations. Each one has been created using the steps previously described. These variations include:

✓ **Pros**	✗ **Cons**
✓ Things we are doing well	✗ Things we could do better
✓ Hopes	✗ Fears
✓ Best-case scenario	✗ Worst-case scenario
✓ Assets	✗ Liabilities
✓ Strengths	✗ Weaknesses
✓ Positives	✗ Negatives
✓ Opportunities	✗ Obstacles

Gap Analysis

What is it? A planning tool that lets groups identify the steps they need to take in order to achieve a goal.

When should you use it? When a group needs to understand the gap between where it currently is and where it ultimately wants to be.

What's its purpose? Gap analysis encourages a realistic review of the present and helps identify the things that need to be done to arrive at the desired future.

What's the outcome? Gap analysis creates a shared view of what needs to be done to eliminate the gap between the present state and the desired future state.

Steps to Do Gap Analysis

1: Identify the future state. Use a tool like visioning or any other approach that generates a picture of where the group wants to be at a specific time. The description of the future must be detailed. Post the information on the right-hand side of a large blank wall.

2: Identify the present state. Meticulously describe the same components featured in the future state, only do so in present terms. Post the ideas generated on the left-hand side of the wall work space.

3: Ask members to work with a partner to identify the gap between the present and the future. Ask questions such as:

> *"What are the gaps between the present and the future?"*

> *"What are the barriers or obstacles to achieving the future?"*

4: Once partners have finished their deliberations, share ideas as a total group and post the gaps between the "present" and the "future."

5: Once there's consensus on the gaps, divide the large group into subgroups. Give each subgroup one or more of the gap items to problem-solve or action-plan.

6: Reassemble the whole group to hear recommendations and action plans. Ask members to ratify the plans, then create a follow-up mechanism.

Gap Analysis

GAP

Present State
Teams operate without leaders for months because there aren't enough people trained

NO team-leader training program

Desired Future
A trained cadre of leaders who can be deployed to support any team

Multi-Voting

What is it? A priority-ranking tool that enables a group to quickly sort through a long list of ideas.

When to use it? After any idea-generating discussion.

What's its purpose? Rapidly establishes priorities in a participative manner. Allows a group to sort a great number of ideas without having to discuss and compare them.

What's the outcome? Multi-voting is democratic and participative. Since most members will see several items they favored near the top of the priority list, multi-voting tends to result in a sense of **I can live with it.**

Steps to Do Multi-Voting

1 : Clarify the items being prioritized. This may be a list of barriers from a force-field analysis or a list of ideas from a brainstorming session. Have members discuss each item to ensure everyone understands the choices.

2 : Identify the voting criteria to ensure that everyone votes with the same criteria in mind. Many situations benefit from voting several times, applying different criteria to each vote. Examples of criteria include:

- o the most important items
- o the lowest-cost items
- o the easiest items to complete
- o the first items in a logical sequence
- o the most innovative items
- o the most significant items given the strategic direction
- o the most important items to our customers

3 : Once the criteria are clear, there are various methods for conducting a multi-vote.

Method 1: Voting with Sticker Dots

o Purchase sheets of file folder dots from an office supply store. Cut the sheets into strips.

o Distribute strips of four to seven dots to each person. Use slightly fewer dots than half the items to be sorted to force people to make choices (for example, give out four dots to sort ten items).

o Ask members to place their stickers on their top four choices. Ensure that no one puts more than one sticker on any one item.

o When everyone has voted, tally the dots in order to arrive at the priorities.

Method 2: Distributing Points

o Give each person points to distribute among the items to be sorted. The number of points is typically either 10 or 100.

o Members then write their points beside the items they favor. It's wise not to allow anyone to place more than 50% of their points on any single item.

o When votes are done, add the scores to arrive at the priorities.

Root-Cause Analysis

What is it? A systematic analysis of an issue to identify the root causes rather than the symptoms.

When should you use it? When you need to delve below surface symptoms and uncover the underlying causes of problems.

What's its purpose? Leads to more complete and final solutions.

What's the outcome? Root-cause analysis enables groups to look more deeply at problems and to deal with the underlying causes. This often means that problems are more likely to be definitively resolved.

Steps to Do Root-Cause Analysis

1: Explain the difference between "causes" and their "effects" to group members. For example, you can ask whether a noisy muffler is a cause or an effect. Once people have identified it as an effect, ask them to list all of the possible causes. Point out that effects can't be solved, but underlying causes can.

2: Use either of the two basic methods for identifying root causes: Cause and Effect Charting or Fishbone Diagrams.

3: Once all causes are identified, brainstorm solutions for each one.

Method 1: Cause and Effect Charting

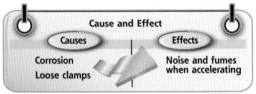

Whenever anyone offers a point of analysis, ask whether it's a cause or an effect. Write each item in its appropriate column. Uncover underlying causes by asking "Why? Why? Why?" about each effect. Continue until all causes have been identified. Use a tool like multi-voting to rank causes.

Method 2: Fishbone Diagrams

A Fishbone Diagram is a visual tool to identify and then sort all of the contributing causes for the situation being analyzed. The cause categories within fishbone charts vary, but usually include people, machinery/equipment, methods, materials, policies, environment, and measurement. The number of categories will vary by subject.

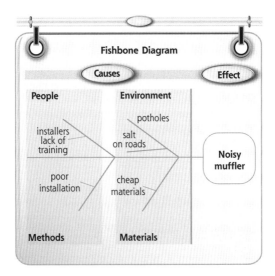

Fishbone Diagram

Causes · Effect

People	Environment
installers lack of training	potholes
	salt on roads
poor installation	cheap materials
Methods	**Materials**

Noisy muffler

Start by placing the observed effect at the "head" of the fishbone. Determine the major cause categories, then ask members to brainstorm all of the possible causes to link to each "rib" of the fish.

Once all of the root causes have been identified, ask the group to brainstorm solutions for each of them, or use multi-voting to sort which causes are the highest priority to solve.

The 5 Whys

What is it? A simple but powerful technique for getting to the root of a problem.

When should you use it? During the analysis step of problem solving.

What's its purpose? To uncover root causes layer by layer.

What's the outcome? Gets past symptoms to the deeper, underlying issues.

Steps to Do the 5 Whys

1: Clarify the symptom that's being explored to ensure that everyone is clear about what's being discussed.

2: Ask the group: "Why is this happening?" Record all responses.

3: Ask: "Why is this happening?" about either the original topic or about the newly recorded information.

4: Repeat the last step three more times, each time recording all comments.

5: Stop to review the notes. Ask members if they think the information generated reflects the root cause of the original issue. If there are multiple root causes identified, you can hand out voting dots and allow members to mark the three to five most significant root causes identified.

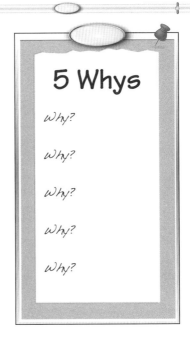

5 Whys

Why?

Why?

Why?

Why?

Why?

A 5 Whys Example:

My car will not start. (problem/symptom)

Why?	The battery is dead.
Why?	The alternator is not functioning.
Why?	The alternator belt has broken.
Why?	The alternator belt is worn out and has never been replaced.
Why?	I don't maintain records of when parts need to be replaced.

Decision Grid

What is it? A matrix of critical criteria used to assess a set of ideas in order to determine which one(s) are most likely to offer the best solution(s).

When should you use it? To bring more objectivity and thoroughness to the decision-making process.

What's its purpose? Changes the decision-making process to one where each potential solution is objectively judged against the same set of criteria.

What's the outcome? Random lists of ideas are systematically sorted. Since everyone gets to cast votes or express opinions, the use of grids engages everyone.

Steps to Do a Decision Grid

Once members have brainstormed a set of ideas, create a decision grid. Two types of decision grids are illustrated below: criteria-based and impact/effort-based.

Criteria-Based Grid

1: Clarify the criteria against which all of the potential solutions will be judged.

Examples:

- saves time
- saves money
- reduces stress
- is timely
- is doable
- is affordable
- is fast

- supports the strategic plan
- is something we can control
- represents the right sequence
- builds empowerment
- will get management support
- satisfies customer needs
- doesn't disrupt our operation

2: The top three to five criteria are chosen from this list and placed along the top of a grid. The options being considered are placed down the left column.

3: Each option is then evaluated as to the extent to which it meets each criterion. Note that some criteria may be more important than others, and are hence given more weight.

> 1 = does not meet the criteria
>
> 2 = somewhat meets the criteria
>
> 3 = good at meeting the criteria

Decision Grid Example:
Decision grid for assessing solutions to the challenge of getting 50 people trained in new software within 14 days.

	Criteria	Cost Effective (x 1)	Meets Customer Needs (x 3)	Speed (x 1)	Lack of Disruption (x 1)	Totals per Solution
Choices	Shut down to give all staff two days' classroom training	1 2 1 1 ÷ 4 = 1.25	1 1 1 1 ÷ 4 = 1.00	3 3 3 3 ÷ 4 = 3.00	1 1 1 1 ÷ 4 = 1.00	**8.25**
	Have experts on site for two weeks to give one-to-one support	2 2 2 1 ÷ 4 = 1.75	2 3 2 2 ÷ 4 = 2.25	1 2 1 1 ÷ 4 = 1.25	3 3 3 3 ÷ 4 = 3.00	**9.25**
	Have only 10 people off for two days at a time	2 2 3 3 ÷ 4 = 2.50	2 3 3 2 ÷ 4 = 2.50	2 2 2 2 ÷ 4 = 2.00	2 2 2 3 ÷ 4 = 2.25	**11.50**

* Four individuals have rated here. The average was calculated by dividing the sum total of the ratings by the number of individuals participating (1 + 2 + 1 + 1 ÷ 4 = 1.25).

** If any of the criteria is more important than the others, it can be given a multiplier factor (i.e., x 3). In the above example, "meets customers needs" is three times more important than the other criteria.

4: Add the scores to determine which solutions will be implemented.

5: Create action plans for top-ranked items.

Impact/Effort-Based Grid

1 : Draw the impact/effort grid on a sheet of flip chart paper.

– EFFORT –
Easy to Do Difficult To Do

	Easy to Do	Difficult To Do
Major Improvement	1	3
Minor Improvement	2	4

– IMPACT –

2 : Discuss the brainstormed ideas one by one and place each in one of the four boxes. All items are eventually classified in the following categories:

1. Easy to do and yields a big improvement
2. Easy to do but yields a small improvement
3. Difficult to do but yields a big improvement
4. Difficult to do and yields small improvement

Category 1 items are implemented immediately.

Category 2 items are also implemented immediately.

Category 3 items are the subject of detailed action planning.

Category 4 items are discarded.

Troubleshooting

What is it? A process for identifying potential blocks and barriers so plans can be formulated to overcome them.

When should you use it? When it's important to identify barriers to success and create action plans to deal with them. When the group has a history of poor follow-through on actions.

What is its purpose? Helps ensure that action plans are well thought out. To improve likelihood of follow-through.

What's the outcome? Groups are less likely to be "surprised" by hidden circumstances, and therefore, gain more control over their work.

Steps to Do Troubleshooting

1: After a group has created action plans, ask members to consider a series of questions. These questions force a critical look at the circumstances that might impede the planned activities. For example:

"What are the difficult, complex, or sensitive aspects of our action plan?"

"What shifts in the environment, like a change of priorities, should we keep our eye on?"

"What organizational blocks or barriers could we encounter?"

"What technical or materials-related problems could stop/delay us?"

"What human resource issues should we anticipate?"

"In what ways might team members not fulfill commitments?"

2: Once potential barriers have been identified, ask members to identify strategies and action plans to overcome each one.

3: Help the group write up its troubleshooting plans. Identify who will monitor follow-through. The following troubleshooting worksheet will help you lead this discussion.

Troubleshooting Worksheet

Planned Activity

What could go wrong, block us, or change suddenly?	What actions do we need to take to overcome each block? (what, how, who, when)

Exit Survey

What is it? An anonymous survey posted near the exit used to take the pulse of a group in order to find out how satisfied members are with overall progress.

When should you use it? At the mid-point of a meeting or workshop. Whenever there's a need to uncover hidden issues and concerns.

What does it do? Provides data about the effectiveness of the meeting or event so that issues can be further explored and addressed. Allows for venting concerns.

What's the outcome? An exit survey acts as a safety valve for releasing anxieties or concerns. It channels concerns into solutions and in this way empowers the group to resolve its own issues.

Steps to Do an Exit Survey

1: Identify two to four questions. Write these on a flip-chart sheet that can be brought forward when the meeting resumes. The following are typical examples of exit survey questions:

Please provide your response to the questions below:

1 = poor   2 = fair   3 = satisfactory   4 = good   5 = excellent

1. Did we achieve what we needed to at today's meeting?

| 1 | 2 | 3 | 4 | 5 |

2. Were everyone's ideas heard and taken into consideration?

| 1 | 2 | 3 | 4 | 5 |

3. Did we make well-thought-out and equitable decisions?

| 1 | 2 | 3 | 4 | 5 |

---

2 : Post the survey sheet on a wall near the exit so group members can mark it as they leave the room. To provide anonymity, place the survey on a flip-chart stand and turn it against the wall to protect the privacy of raters. Provide markers and ask people to rate each survey item.

3 : At the start of the next session with that group, review the exit survey sheet. Use the survey feedback process on the next page to address each item.

4 : At the end of the discussion, review improvement ideas. These will fall into two categories: action steps and new norms. The new norms should be added to the existing norms for this team. Conduct exit surveys periodically as a preventative means of keeping meetings running effectively.

Survey Feedback

What is it? A process that involves gathering information and feeding it back to members so that they can interpret the data and identify action steps.

When should you use it? When there's a problem that group members need to address about which they lack information. Can be implemented when a problem has been identified. Can also be used periodically as a preventative measure.

What's its purpose? Provides the group with a means of assessing the efficiency and effectiveness of a meeting or activity. Also provides a method for generating actions to resolve any identified problems.

What's the outcome? Creates a sense of commitment and accountability among members for making improvements. Acts as a catalyst for making improvements.

Steps to Do Survey Feedback

1: Design and conduct a survey. This can take an anonymous form or be an open process, such as an exit survey. The survey can be about:

- o meeting effectiveness
- o team/group effectiveness
- o leader performance
- o process effectiveness
- o customer satisfaction
- o a recent event or project

2: After the surveys have been individually completed, they're returned to a designated member of the group. This person tabulates the survey results by combining all of the responses onto a blank survey form. The person doing the tabulation doesn't interpret the results; he or she only combines the ratings from the individual surveys.

3: Tabulated survey results are fed back to the group. After members have had an opportunity to read the results, two categories of questions are posed:

1. *"What does the survey data tell us is going well? Which items received high ratings? Why did these items receive high ratings?"*

2. *"What does the survey data tell us are problems or issues? Which items received low ratings? Why did these items receive low ratings?"*

4: Once members have identified the items that received sufficiently low ratings to be of concern, have them rank these in terms of priority to determine which should be addressed.

5 : Once the top priorities are clear, divide the members into subgroups of no fewer than four individuals. Give each subgroup one issue to work on for twenty to thirty minutes. Deal with as many issues as group size allows. In subgroups, members will answer two sets of questions about the item they have been given:

1. *"Why did this item get a low rating? What's wrong here? What is the nature of the problem?"* (Group members analyze the problem.)

2. *"What are possible solutions for this problem? What will remedy the situation?"* (Members generate solutions.)

6 : Reassemble the total group and ask subgroups to share their recommendations. Encourage everyone to add their ideas and to ratify their final actions. Select the best ideas and implement them.

7 : Ask members to briefly return to their subgroups to complete any action plans that might be needed to ensure that improvements are implemented.

Needs and Offers Dialogue

What is it? A constructive dialogue between two parties to identify action steps they can take to improve their relationship. A positive and constructive dialogue that lets people express past and present concerns about the relationship in totally constructive terms.

When should you use it? To encourage dialogue between parties to either resolve a conflict or improve relations proactively before problems occur.

What's its purpose? To vent concerns and resolve interpersonal issues in a low-risk manner. To negotiate a new, more positive relationship.

What's the outcome? An improved understanding of each other's views and feelings. Mutual agreement to action plans that will enhance relations.

Steps to Do a Needs and Offers Dialogue

1: Clarify who will be the focus of the exercise. This can be a team and its leader, two subgroups of the same team, a team and management, or two individuals.

2: Set a positive climate for the exercise by talking about the value of giving and receiving feedback. Make sure that the appropriate norms are in place to encourage members to speak freely and honestly.

3: Explain the rules of the exercise. The two parties will be separated for a period of twenty to thirty minutes. During that time, each party will identify what he or she needs from the other party in order to be effective. This process is identical whether the parties are two individuals or a team and its leader.

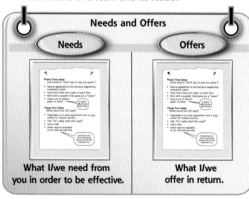

4: When each party has written its "needs list," bring the parties back together to share their thoughts, one at a time. While one party is sharing his or her needs, the other must listen actively, then provide a summary of the other party's needs.

Facilitation at a Glance! | Fourth Edition | ©2018 GOAL/QPC

5 : Once parties have heard and acknowledged each other's needs, separate them again for twenty or thirty minutes while they consider what they're prepared to offer to the other party.

6 : Bring the parties back together and have them take turns sharing their offers. Allow for discussions of clarification. End the conversation by having members ratify what they have heard and make commitments to follow through.

Gallery Walk

What is it? A safe and participative means of engaging a large number of people in productive conversations about specific issues. A way of using the walls in a room to gain a lot of input from a large group in a short time.

When should you use it? When you want to explore a wide range of topics with a large number of people and have little time to do it. To energize a group and bring everyone into the conversation. When there is a topic that people may not want to talk about in open conversation. When a large open space with useable walls is available and you have a group of at least twenty people.

What does it do? Creates a relatively safe and anonymous setting for conversation. Provides an alternative means of generating group synergy because people read and then build on each other's ideas.

What's the outcome? A large number of issues are explored. Group ideas are developed. Everyone participates and their ideas are added into the mix.

Steps to Do a Gallery Walk

1 : Set up the room by posting blank sheets of flip-chart paper in separate locations around the room. Electronic boards can also be used.

---

2 : Clarify the topic or series of topics to be discussed. Then divide the topic into segments or sub-topics.

3 : Post one topic segment or sub-topic at the top of its own flip-chart sheet.

4 : Instruct people to wander the room and gather at a flip chart that features a topic about which they have knowledge. Be clear that there must always be no fewer than three and no more than five people at each flip chart. Once there, the participants discuss the topic and record their collective thoughts for a specified period, typically about five minutes.

5 : At the end of five minutes invite everyone to wander to another flip chart station, read what the first group has written, and confer with whomever else wandered there in order to add more comments to the sheet. This process can be repeated until all of the flip-chart sheets are filled. It is not necessary for each person to visit each station.

Gallery Walk variations and applications:

In planning exercises, the flip chart topics can coincide with various key questions in the planning process, such as: What are the key consumer trends. What competitive forces do we face. What are our manufacturing strengths? What are our manufacturing weaknesses? What are the next technological innovations we need to prepare to adopt? and so forth.

In a problem-solving exercise, it's possible to solve a large number of problems by posting each in a different area and then having participants wander to initially analyze each problem. When all of the problems have been analyzed by at least three sets of wandering visitors, have people retrace their steps to read the completed analysis sheets and then begin to brainstorm solutions. After everyone has wandered to at least three stations to add solutions,

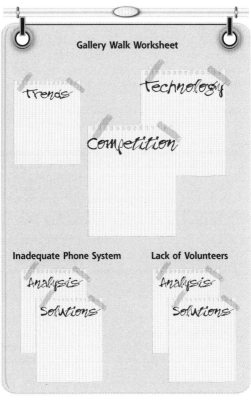

Gallery Walk Worksheet

Trends

Technology

Competition

Inadequate Phone System

Analysis

Solutions

Lack of Volunteers

Analysis

Solutions

give each participant a colored marker and invite the participants to tour all of the sheets of brainstormed solutions to check off the three ideas they think should be implemented.

Systematic Problem Solving

What is it? A step-by-step approach for resolving a problem or issue.

When should you use it? When members need to work together to solve a problem.

What's its purpose? Provides a structured and disciplined means for groups to explore and resolve an issue together. In-depth analysis ensures that groups understand the problem before jumping to solutions.

What's the outcome? Systematic problem solving results in doable action steps that members of the group take responsibility for implementing. Because the process is systematic, it discourages members from randomly suggesting ideas. Problem solving is at the heart of collaborative conflict resolution. It's also a key activity in any organization that is dedicated to improving its processes and service to customers.

Steps to Do Systematic Problem Solving

1 : **Name the problem.** Identify a problem that needs to be solved. Analyze it briefly to ensure that there's a common understanding of the issue. Then support the group in writing a one- or two-sentence description of the problem. This is called the problem statement.

2 : **Identify the goal of the problem-solving exercise.** Ask the group questions such as: "If this problem were totally solved, how would you describe the ideal situation?" or "How will things look if we solve this problem?" Summarize this in a one- to two-sentence goal statement.

3 : **Analyze the problem.** If the problem is fairly technical, do a detailed analysis using a Fishbone Diagram (see Chapter Ten). Otherwise, ask a series of probing questions to help members think analytically about

the problem. Categorize the observations as either "causes" or "effects." The goal is to get to underlying root causes of the problem. Some useful questions during analysis could include:

- Describe this problem to me in detail, step by step.
- What is it? How does it manifest itself?
- What are the noticeable signs of it?
- What makes this happen?
- How are people affected?
- What other problems does it cause?
- What are the most damaging aspects?
- What stops us from solving it?
- Who gets in the way of solving it?
- What are the root causes of each symptom?

4: **Identify potential solutions.** Use brainstorming or written brainstorming to generate potential solutions. When the ideas stop flowing, ask probing questions to encourage members to dig deeper. Some useful probing questions include:

- What if money were no object?
- What if you owned this company?
- What would the customer suggest?
- What if we did the opposite of the ideas suggested so far?
- What is the most innovative thing we could do?

5: **Evaluate solutions.** Use multi-voting, a criterion-based decision grid, or an impact/effort grid to sift through the brainstormed ideas to determine which are most applicable to the situation.

6: **Create an action plan.** Identify the specific steps needed to implement the chosen solutions. Specify how things will be done, when, and by whom. Each action step should also feature performance indicators that answer the question, "*How will we know we have been successful?*" This will help focus the action step and make it easier to measure results.

7: **Troubleshoot the plan.** Use the troubleshooting worksheet to identify all of the things that could get in the way and then ensure that there are plans in place to deal with them.

8: **Monitor and evaluate.** Identify how the action plans will be monitored and when and how the results will be reported on. Create and use a monitoring and report-back format.

Systematic Problem Solving Step 1

1: Name the Problem

Identify the problem that needs to be solved. Analyze it in just enough detail to create a common understanding. Explore the general nature of the problem on paper.

Then narrow in and select the specific aspect you wish to solve. Write a one- or two-sentence problem statement to define the problem clearly.

Systematic Problem Solving Step 2

2: Identify the Goal of the Problem-Solving Exercise

Describe the desired outcome. Ask: "*What would things look like if the problem disappeared? How would things look if this problem were resolved?*"

Record the ideas generated. Then narrow in and write a one- or two-sentence goal statement.

Systematic Problem Solving Step 3

3: Analyze the Problem

Dissect the problem thoroughly. Avoid coming up with solutions. Instead, concentrate on making sure that everyone is clear about the specific nature of the situation. Don't focus on symptoms, but delve behind each effect to determine the root causes.

Use a fishbone diagram if the problem is a complex technical issue that has many contributing factors. If it isn't a mechanical problem, use cause and effect charting by asking:

"How would we describe this problem to an outsider?"

"What is taking place? What are the signs and symptoms?"

"How are people affected? What makes this happen?"

"What are the root causes of each symptom?"

"What are the most damaging aspects?"

Systematic Problem Solving Step 4

4: Identify Potential Solutions

Use brainstorming or anonymous brainstorming to generate a range of potential solutions to the problem. When brainstorming, remember the rules:

- Let ideas flow; be creative, don't judge
- All ideas are good, even if they're way-out
- Build on the ideas of others

Questions to ask once the initial flow of ideas has stopped:

"What if money were no object or I owned the company?"

"What would the customer suggest?"

"What's the opposite of something already suggested?"

"What is the most innovative thing we could do?"

Systematic Problem Solving Step 5

5 : Evaluate the Solutions

Use multi-voting, a criterion-based decision grid, or the impact/effort grid shown below to sort through the brainstormed ideas and identify a course of action.

<table>
<tr>
<td></td>
<td></td>
<td colspan="2" style="text-align:center">– EFFORT –
Easy to Do   Difficult to Do</td>
</tr>
<tr>
<td rowspan="2">– IMPACT –</td>
<td>Major
Improvement</td>
<td style="text-align:center">1</td>
<td style="text-align:center">3</td>
</tr>
<tr>
<td>Minor
Improvement</td>
<td style="text-align:center">2</td>
<td style="text-align:center">4</td>
</tr>
</table>

Course of Action

List all of the Type 1 & 2 activities together for quick action	List all of the Type 3 activities for development into action plans

Systematic Problem Solving Step 6

6 : Plan for Action

Create detailed action plans for items to be implemented. Ensure that action plans adhere to a logical sequence of steps. Provide details about what will be done, how, and by whom. Always include target dates for completion. Identify the performance indicator that answers the question: *"How will we know we did a good job?"*

Action Plan			
What will be done & how?	**By whom?**	**When?**	**Performance indicator**

Systematic Problem Solving Step 7

7: Troubleshoot the Action Plan

Identify the things in the way of successful implementation of the action plan. Create anticipatory strategies to deal with each blockage. Identify trouble spots by asking questions such as:

"What are the most difficult, complex, or sensitive aspects of the plan?"

"What sudden shifts could take place to change priorities or otherwise change the environment?"

"What organizational blocks and barriers could we run into?"

"What technical or materials-related problems could stop/delay us?"

"Should we be aware of any human resources issues? If so, which ones?"

"How could members of this team not fulfill their commitments?"

Course of Action

List all of the things that could hinder or block progress	Identify what can be done to overcome these blocks

Systematic Problem Solving Step 8

8 : Monitor and Evaluate

To ensure action plans are actually implemented, answer the following questions:

How will progress be reported?

Written _____

Verbal _____

When and how often will reports be made? _____

Who needs to be informed? _____

How will results be monitored? _____

Will there be a final report? _____

Who will take responsibility for actions? _____

Reporting on Results

Implemented activities	What results have been achieved?
Remaining items	Expected dates for completion

FACILITATORS SPEND AS MUCH TIME CREATING THEIR PROCESS NOTES FOR A MEETING AS THEY SPEND ACTUALLY FACILITATING THE DIALOGUE.

Chapter

ELEVEN

Meeting Design Template

Meetings are complex activities that always need to be carefully designed. Facilitators conduct careful assessments and write detailed meeting design notes before they facilitate complex meetings.

Experienced facilitators typically create several different design options before deciding on the one to use. By considering different approaches, facilitators build in options and flexibility in case the initial approach proves to be ineffective.

Steps in meeting design:

❑ the facilitator reviews data collected from site visits, background reading, interviews, surveys, focus groups, and process observation

❑ the facilitator identifies key meeting elements and prepares a final draft of the proposed agenda

❑ group members are invited to comment on the design and recommend changes

❑ a final design is created and sent to members for ratification

❑ a meeting agenda is prepared and circulated to members before the meeting.

Challenges of this step:

❑ making an accurate assessment of the data

❑ identifying the appropriate goal and objectives/outcomes

❑ identifying effective process elements

❑ correctly sequencing the activities

❑ helping members overcome their resistance to specific elements of the design

❑ being open to changes suggested by group members

❑ creating a flexible design that can be adjusted to match meeting dynamics.

Potential pitfalls of meeting design:

❑ hasty, inadequate data review

❑ underestimating the blocks and barriers

❑ deliberately ignoring difficult aspects

❑ failing to build in activities to overcome blocks or create needed norms

❑ planning activities that are inappropriate for the group

❑ not planning alternative activities in case an element in the original design proves to be ineffective.

Meeting Design Template
Use the following series of questions to help you in the design process.

1. What is the overall goal of the facilitation activity?

2. What are the objectives and expected outcomes of the session?

Objectives		**Expected Outcomes**
i. _____		_____
ii. _____		_____
iii. _____		_____
iv. _____		_____

3. Who should ideally attend?

4. What homework do participants need to do?

5. Does the group need a warm-up exercise to build familiarity or break the ice? If so, what should be its purpose and length?

6. What's the nature of the conversations that need to be part of this meeting? Assign a time percentage to each:

    ___ % that will be information sharing

    ___ % that will be planning discussions

    ___ % that will be problem-solving activities

    ___ % that will be relationship-building conversations

7. Describe the decisions that need to be made. How difficult is each decision? What level of empowerment is appropriate for each decision item?

Describe the decisions that need to be made	Difficulty level? (1 = low, 5 = high)	Empowerment level? (I, II, III, IV)

8. Is there likely to be resistance? If so, what buy-in question(s) or targeted norming question(s) should be asked to overcome that resistance?

9. What else might go wrong during the facilitation? What challenges should you anticipate?

10. What will you say to clarify your role? Who else needs to have his or her role clarified?

11. What specific norming questions need to be asked in order to create the most effective climate for the session?

12. What questions will you ask during a mid-point check?

13. What questions will you post on the exit survey at the end of the meeting?

Meeting Components at a Glance

Activity	Process Elements
Welcome and Overview	Welcome to leaders
	Feedback of survey data
	Review of goal, objectives, and outcomes
	Agenda overview
Warm-up Activities	Small group or partner discussions
	Personal introductions
	Structured group games
Needs Assessment	Entrance surveys
	Wandering flip charts
	Posing key questions
Presentations	Briefings about new developments
	Briefings about new products
	Training sessions
Information Sharing	Round-robin sharing of updates
Planning Problem Solving	Visioning/goal setting
	Environmental scans
	SWOT analysis
	Benchmarking
	Strategy development
	Implementation planning
Relationship Building	Personal goal setting
	Sharing personal information
	Building a team profile
	Team goal setting
	Team work planning
	Needs and offers dialogues
	Interpersonal mediations
	Peer feedback
	Celebrating success
Evaluation	Establishing expected outcomes
	Verbal process checks
	Written exit surveys
	Meeting evaluation sheets
	Posted exit surveys

INDEX

Notes

GOALQPC
uality

How to Use Our Pocket Guides

Designed for you to use as a convenient and quick reference guide on the job or on the go. Our concise format, is crucial for understanding and retention of the tools. Put your finger on any individual tool or process within seconds!

Use this guide as part of a self-study program or as a reference before, during, and after your training to learn the different types of tools and their uses. Workshops offer the highest rate of educational retention. Host a workshop for hands-on practice.

By the Same Author - Conflict At A Glance!

Conflict will find you, whether you're ready and equipped to handle it, or not!

Don't leave it to chance how you deal with your everyday disagreements, long-established rifts, and out-and-out battles. A quick read of Conflict at a Glance! will help you understand common types of conflicts, body language, ineffective and effective dialog, and the power of good listening skills. You'll learn the simple steps of a conflict management approach, whether you are cultivating a new mindset and way of interacting as a supervisor or as a member of a team or community group, or if you are mediating a dispute between other people.

Benefits:

This book is a working toolbox with real-world examples, checklists, self-tests, and tips. It fully describes 14 techniques for resolving disputes, (while still maintaining relationships), and six tactics for neutralizing toxic behaviors. It may well become a reference-at-the-ready in your pocket, briefcase, or pocketbook. This is an essential resource for:

- Managers, team/project leaders
- Customer service professionals
- Community members and members of social groups
- Family members, married couples and parents
- Principals, teachers and students
- Anyone who must maintain a good relationship with family, workers and supervisors, vendors and customers

available from GOALQPC at
www.goalpqc.com

Make it Your Own

Take any Pocket Guide and apply your company's own personal style. Customization allows you to creatively combine the contents of GOAL/QPC products with your own documents and training materials.

Include your motto, mission, and logo on the outside and inside covers, and even add your own illustrations and text. Communicate your organization's approach by including other tools, internal problem-solving processes, or your organization's strategic initiatives.

Contact us today for a no obligation quote.
800.643.4316 | 603.893.1944
service@goalqpc.com | GOALQPC.com
MemoryJogger.org